LIFE

OUR CALL TO ARMS

The Attack on Pearl Harbor

A tale of three battleships: Rescue boats from the *Maryland* (left) surrounded the sunken *Oklahoma* (hull visible at right). In the background, the *West Virginia* was in flames.

LIFE

OUR CALL TO ARMS

The Attack on Pearl Harbor

Editor Robert Sullivan

Art Director Ian Denning

Picture Editor
Barbara Baker Burrows

Senior Editor Robert Andreas

Associate Picture Editors
Donna F. Aceto,
Cornelia Jackson

Senior Writer Daniel S. Levy

Senior Reporter
Hildegard Anderson

Contributing Editors
Charles Hirshberg,
Tim Larimer, Richard Schickel

Copy Chief Erikka Haa

Production Manager
Michael H. Roseman

Picture Researchers
Joan Shweky, Lauren Steel

Copy Editor Zoë Rosenfeld

Business Manager
Edward Nana Osei-Bonsu

We would like to express our grateful appreciation to the following:
Picture editor Suzanne Hodgart; Admiral Nimitz Museum and Historical Center; American Folklife Center, the Library of Congress; Judith Bowman, U.S. Army Museum of Hawaii; DeSoto Brown, Bishop Museum; Dudley Harris; Bill Hooper; Hawaii State Archives; National Japanese American Memorial Foundation; Naval Historical Center; Special Collections Department, Joyner Library, East Carolina University; Stan Cohen, Pictorial Histories; University of North Texas, Oral History Collection; USS Arizona Memorial, NPS.

We also relied on numerous written sources and would especially like to acknowledge our debt to:
At Dawn We Slept: The Untold Story of Pearl Harbor by Gordon W. Prange, and *Day of Infamy* by Walter Lord.

**Time Inc.
Home Entertainment**

President Rob Gursha

**Vice President,
Branded Businesses**
David Arfine

**Executive Director,
Marketing Services**
Carol Pittard

**Director, Retail & Special
Sales** Tom Mifsud

Director of Finance
Tricia Griffin

Marketing Directors
Kenneth Maehlum,
Maarten Terry

Assistant Director
Ann Marie Ross

**Editorial Operations
Manager** John Calvano

**Associate Product
Managers** Jennifer
Dowell, Meredith Shelley

**Assistant Product
Manager** Michelle Kuhr

Special thanks to: Victoria Alfonso, Suzanne DeBenedetto, Robert Dente, Gina Di Meglio, Peter Harper, Roberta Harris, Natalie McCrea, Jessica McGrath, Jonathan Polsky, Emily Rabin, Mary Jane Rigoroso, Steven Sandonato, Tara Sheehan, Bozena Szwagulinski, Marina Weinstein, Niki Whelan

Copyright 2001
Time Inc. Home Entertainment

Published by

Time Inc.
1271 Avenue of the Americas
New York, New York 10020

All rights reserved. No part of this book may be reproduced in any form or by any electronic or mechanical means, including information storage and retrieval systems, without permission in writing from the publisher, except by a reviewer, who may quote brief passages in a review.

First Edition

ISBN: 1-929049-32-3
Library of Congress
Catalogue Number:
2001087958
"LIFE" is a trademark of
Time Inc.

We welcome your comments and suggestions about LIFE Books. Please write to us at:
LIFE Books
Attention: Book Editors
PO Box 11016
Des Moines, IA 50336-1016

If you would like to order any of our hardcover Collector's Edition books, please call us at 1-800-327-6388. (Monday through Friday, 7:00 a.m. – 8:00 p.m., or Saturday, 7:00 a.m. – 6:00 p.m. Central Time.)

Please visit our website at
www.TimeBookstore.com

PRINTED IN THE UNITED
STATES OF AMERICA

Sailors at Kaneohe Bay tried to beach a PBY Catalina that had been strafed early in the attack. A later strike would finish off the reconnaissance seaplane.

U.S. Navy

Introduction by Hugh Sidey

On the day after the attack, stunned Americans were eager for anything that might shed light on the terrible new world they now inhabited. Here, the Embassy Newsreel theater in New York City was a magnet for passersby hoping to see images from Pearl Harbor—or anywhere else that might suddenly have become important.

Pearl Harbor is the story of the worst battle defeat ever suffered by the U.S., and of how courage and ingenuity rose from the smoldering wreckage to build the world's most powerful war machine and, in victory's aftermath, to wage peace with even greater scope and success.

There—the Territory of Hawaii—and then—December 7, 1941—came towering explosions, monstrous ships moaning as they died, lithe young sailors trapped in steel hulks. Here—the continental 48 states—we got radio bulletins in the middle of Sunday music, pot roast on hold and cooling. It was the end of harangues by Charles Lindbergh, the world's most famous person, and his bellowing followers that America should stay out of foreign wars. He joined the crusade and eventually he fought, as did 15 million other men and women.

We knew war was coming. As a teenager in a small Iowa town, I was surrounded by men who had charged through Belleau Wood and the Meuse-Argonne in 1918 to subdue the Kaiser. For two years these veterans had talked about "fighting the Hun again." I'd watched the headlines of Nazi conquest. The draft had long been under way.

But the war came another way.

My mother called up the stairs as I was taking off my good clothes. "Japan has attacked us. It means we are at war." I stood pantless for other shouted bulletins. (Over the years I have been amused by how many friends were also caught awkwardly in the ritual church-to-play transition.) We had been aware of the tension with Japan, but only vaguely. It was so distant, both geographically and culturally.

My brother was drying the Sunday dinner dishes, repeating words from the radio: "Honolulu … Pearl Harbor … " They were almost meaningless to me—and to most Americans. One of the singing Andrews Sisters, on tour in Cincinnati, asked, "Where is Pearl Harbor?" In Washington a State Department "expert" thought it was in the Philippines. Novelist William Styron, then a boy, heard a Virginia waitress reporting that the Japanese had bombed Pearl Harbor. "Imagine them gettin' all the way to South Carolina," she said. The officer who relayed the flash to British Prime Minister Winston Churchill was equally perplexed. He asked that Pearl Harbor be spelled out. And the number of U.S. military leaders at parties, football games and out horseback riding, though there was evidence of a possible attack in the intelligence system, was appalling.

The Pearl Harbor moment would become above all others—until the assassination of John Kennedy—the nation's mental freeze-frame. Andover senior

Just as JFK's death would be inextricably linked to TV images for most people, so was the news of Pearl Harbor a radio memory (left, NBC's New York newsroom). Right: Invasion fever spread across the country, particularly along the coasts. Note the headline in this December 9 edition of New York's *The Sun*.

George H.W. Bush would remember how shocked he had been. Only a few months before, he had entertained thoughts of enlisting in the Canadian Air Force to fight with the British in European skies. Now he could find his way to battle in service to the U.S. He would in three years be shot down on a torpedo run against the Japanese.

Thirty years after Pearl Harbor a new neighbor of mine, retired Air Force Maj. Gen. Brooke Allen, leaned over my back fence in Maryland and spoke quietly of his desperate drive in 1941 to gather his crew and get to his B-17, parked on Hickam Field. He ducked behind a bulldozer to escape the strafing Zeros, bullets pinging off the blade. He watched the deadly stream chop off the head of a sprinting airman. He got a bomber off the ground—one of only two to escape.

Richard L. Strout, a legendary newsman for the *Christian Science Monitor,* told me that Pearl Harbor marked the lowest point for the U.S. in his 60 years of reporting in Washington. "The fleet was destroyed; Hitler was still subduing Europe. The prospects were bleak." Strout knew that Franklin Roosevelt and many of his people were meeting on that afternoon to somehow confront the disaster. He walked over to the White House and stood on the lawn, mute in the cold, with thousands of others. "Then someone began singing 'God Bless America' and we all joined. That changed things. I felt we'd come through."

Adolf Hitler felt otherwise. "Now," he exulted, "we cannot lose the war!" Winston Churchill rightly reckoned that Pearl Harbor would thrust the U.S. directly into the war and assure a victory for the Allies, no matter how difficult the road ahead. Japanese Admiral Yamamoto Isoroku, who planned and launched the surprise Pearl Harbor attack, also knew the awesome challenge Japan faced despite this opening triumph. Yamamoto had been a naval attaché in Washington from 1926 to 1928 and had traveled the U.S., studying the country's productive capacity. He warned his fellow warriors that military action must be swift and intimidating in order to persuade America to reach some kind of agreement for peace. Otherwise, the U.S. would build overwhelming and irresistible strength. Pearl Harbor, despite the humiliation and momentary terror it caused America, did not produce the victory Yamamoto envisioned.

More important, Gen. George C. Marshall, the U.S.'s top military man, understood that the war would ultimately be won on the farms and in the factories of the nation. In just four years he would gather a huge army, train it and supply it with, among other things, 88,410 tanks, 4,490,000 bayonets, 469,000,000 pounds of cabbage—and, finally, two atomic bombs.

Pearl Harbor, in its awful treachery and death, unfettered a human miracle of spirit and mind that carries us on today.

The Nazis were obsessed with military panoply and symbolism, a fact much in evidence when Der Führer saluted the crowd in Adolf Hitler Platz during the Nuremberg Reich's Party Congress in 1938.

Hugo Jaeger

1 | HITLER'S DRUMBEAT

The accords of Versailles, drawn up in the aftermath of World War I, so severely punished Germany that the response was bound to go beyond resentment. Eventually there would be small rebellions, at the least, perhaps even stabs at revolution. These things did come to pass, but still—no one could have foreseen that from the ashes of the Great War an Adolf Hitler would rise. He seemed, by turns, a loser, a petty radical, a thug, a threat and, finally, a vanquishing force to be dealt with. Yet by the time democracies paid Hitler the attention he required, it was too late. With Hitler marching, the world was being violently and forever altered. And as he set fire after fire throughout Europe, America was drawn ever closer to the flames.

German troops marched closer to war when they entered Czechoslovakia in October 1938, just days after the Munich agreement, whereby Britain and France ceded the Czech region of the Sudetenland to Germany. Eight months earlier, Hitler had annexed Austria, then turned his attention to the Sudeten area, which, prior to the treaties of Versailles and St.-Germain, had been German for centuries. It didn't take long for these Sudetens to adopt the Nazi salute.

The first seeds of World War II were sown on June 28, 1919, when France and Britain carried the day and their version of the Treaty of Versailles was signed by representatives of the Great War's victors. Any conciliation offered by U.S. President Woodrow Wilson was scorned—even mocked—as Europe's two standing powers wanted not merely peace but punishment. They carved up Germany, ceding to Czechoslovakia, for example, the Sudetenland, a large part of which clearly wished to stay German because it *was* German—in heritage, language and blood. Then England and France sought to wreck what remained of Germany by ordering monetary reparations that were as heedless of consequence as they were impossible to meet. "The policy of reducing Germany to servitude for a generation, of degrading the lives of millions of human beings, and of depriving a whole nation of happiness should be abhorrent and detestable," the economist John Maynard Keynes wrote one year after the treaty was signed. France and Britain said the policy represented just deserts.

However, while the Versailles pact was meant to all but vaporize the German state, it had precisely the opposite effect.

Germany, careening toward economic collapse, grew desperate. Wild inflation brought down the Weimar Republic, while strikes and socialist revolts erupted throughout the land. Various saviors put themselves forth, but none matched the charisma, will and message of Adolf Hitler. A Great War veteran who said that Germany's way out of its quagmire was defense, defiance and national pride, he laid claim in his speeches to land that had been reapportioned. Versailles had stipulated for Germany a maximum of 100,000 standing troops and no air force. Hitler, having been named chancellor

Hutton Getty Archive/Liaison

Axis Aggressors

Each man called himself The Leader: **Benito Mussolini** was Il Duce, and **Adolf Hitler** was Der Führer. These longtime dictators of Japan's two partners in the Axis (a term coined by Mussolini) had more than a name in common. Hitler came to power in 1933, 11 years later than Mussolini, whom he deeply admired. Both had made rapid ascents in countries that once flourished mightily but, in the wake of World War I, were left shattered physically and spiritually.

To reverse their nations' fortunes, both men resorted to—and became synonymous with— fascism. They attained their goals with armies of brown- and black-shirted goons who devoured their brilliant oratory, which was malevolent and often erroneous yet hypnotically dramatic and vibrant. As heads of state they enjoyed some early success, notably in creating employment that helped overcome widespread poverty, but their frenzied xenophobia and racism (traits equally abundant in Tokyo) overshadowed their achievements.

For a while, Mussolini was cool to entering into a drawn-out conflict; when he saw the spoils of war accruing to Hitler, however, he caught the fever and, in 1940, dragged his unprepared country into the fray. Mussolini's desire to be the next Caesar would lead to a gruesome public display of his corpse in a Milan square. Hitler's need to be greater than any Caesar would lead to a seedy Berlin bunker and some charred remains.

Blood brothers Hitler and Mussolini enjoyed a motor tour of Florence, Italy, in May 1938.

Hulton Getty Archive/Liaison

German bombers blasted Warsaw in September 1939, marking the advent of World War II. The Poles, caught off-guard by the blitzkrieg tactics, fought valiantly but to no avail. By the end of the year, Germany and the Soviet Union had divided Poland between them.

in 1933—a month before Franklin D. Roosevelt was sworn in as U.S. President—re-armed, blatantly snubbing the accords. The League of Nations in general, and Britain and France in particular, did nothing to stop him, consumed as they were with their own economic troubles. Suddenly Hitler, and a reborn Germany, were at the table.

September 1, 1939: Germany invaded Poland; two days later, France and Britain declared war on Germany. Two weeks later, the Soviet Union, which had recently entered into a nonaggression pact with Hitler, also invaded Poland. The country was taken by month's end.

While Japan was busy extending its dominion in the East, Germany and the U.S.S.R. had designs on all of Europe. In November 1939, Moscow began waging the Winter War in Finland and was victorious by spring. Between April and early June, Germany swept through Denmark, Norway, the Netherlands and Belgium. Both aggressors heard, if faintly, protests from America—a moral embargo against

the Soviets, scoldings for Hitler—but they also read the foreign polls, which showed that more than half of the U.S. public didn't want to offer even financial assistance to the besieged nations. Hitler wasn't worried about American intervention in the war because the U.S. military, like its society, was weak by nature, polluted, as he saw it, by so much African and Jewish blood.

Germany's troops were poised at the Maginot Line, the supposedly impregnable defensive fortifications on France's northeastern border. On May 10, 1940, Prime Minister Neville Chamberlain of Great Britain resigned; his earlier appeasement of Hitler had proved a disaster. Winston Churchill became the commonwealth's leader, declaring, "I have nothing to offer but blood, toil, tears and sweat." Over the next several years, the U.S. and Great Britain would both be fortunate to have leaders who, when the going got tough, could offer inspiration, determination and courage.

On May 12, Germany attacked France. A month

National Archives

London Times

It was mid-1940, and things looked bleak for Britain. In a London suburb, children sat on the rubble of what was their home, fearing another night of German bombing. Above: British and French troops formed endless lines waiting to vacate Dunkirk's beaches. Getting the men out of France was a moral victory, but as Churchill said, "wars are not won by evacuations."

later, Italy declared war on both France and Britain. France fell on June 22, and within a week Charles de Gaulle, a tall, charismatic general who had escaped to England, was named head of the underground Free French movement. On July 10, the Battle of Britain began. Hitler, having conquered one of the tormentors of Versailles, was out to vanquish the other.

And what does this have to do with Pearl Harbor?

The U.S. was watching Europe keenly and was intent on helping Britain survive. Meanwhile, America was working through negotiations to keep a dicey situation in the East from degenerating. Neither the U.S. war machine nor the American public was ready to engage in battle, but both figured that if push came to shove, it would happen in Europe. The idea that the first blow would be struck by Japan was not yet anticipated.

Roosevelt felt that war was imminent and accordingly took steps to ensure that his country was prepared. On December 17, 1940, he spoke metaphorically of America's relationship to beleaguered Britain, asking whether, with a neighbor's house on fire, we shouldn't lend a garden hose and seek no payment in return. Speaking to his countrymen during one of his famous fireside chats after Christmas, he asserted: "We must admit that there is a risk in any course we may take. But I deeply believe that the great majority of our people agree that the course that I advocate involves the least risk now and the greatest hope for world peace in the future. ... We must be the great arsenal of democracy."

The speeches had a galvanizing effect; suddenly a majority of the American public would risk the consequences of heightened involvement (short of a commitment of troops) in order to support Britain. The course that Roosevelt advocated, in the near term, was made manifest as House Bill 1776—the "Declaration of Interdependence," or more commonly, Lend-Lease. Even if U.S. soldiers wouldn't yet march off to war, U.S. munitions would, in quantity. As ships and guns arrived in England, Churchill called Lend-Lease a "new Magna Carta."

By 1941, Japan, knowing that it was embarking on risky business in the Pacific, had secured for itself a place in the Tripartite Pact with Germany and Italy. Under the terms of the deal, if any of the partners was attacked by a nation not yet in the war, the others would hurry to its aid. The Axis was formed.

The Allies, in the meantime, were also joined by another major partner. On June 22, Hitler stunned the world by roaring into Russia—breaking his

In August 1941, off the coast of Newfoundland, FDR and Churchill met for the first time, and the prime minister again pressed for aid. Above, they bade farewell aboard the USS *Augusta*, before the British leader was piped over the side, at right. Churchill would later say, "No lover ever studied every whim of his mistress as I did those of President Roosevelt."

nonaggression pact. A month later the Luftwaffe was raking Moscow from the air. All summer and through the fall, the Nazis pressed on, winning battle after battle, overrunning towns, taking as many as 2 million Russians prisoner. By late 1941, the fascists had under their boots more than 330 million people in a region that stretched from the west coast of Spain to the outskirts of Moscow.

Britain, however, survived. The Blitz had failed—the first slowing of the German march. There was still a chance, Churchill felt. If only America would enter the war.

Even as the U.S. Congress debated repeal of the 1939 Neutrality Act in autumn 1941, a U.S. destroyer, the *Kearney,* was torpedoed in the Atlantic by a German U-boat and limped back to port. Although there had been earlier torpedo and depth-charge exchanges involving American ships, Roosevelt said, ominously, "History has recorded who fired the first shot."

But the *Kearney* incident was not enough. The United States would be drawn into the war only by something much bigger.

In July 1938, Japanese troops invaded a village in China's Anhui province. Japan already controlled China's main cities and much of its coastline.

AP/Wide World

2 | THUNDER IN THE EAST

In the 1930s, Japan had its own expansionist intentions—in China, first, then deep into the Pacific. The vastness of the empire's reach led, by necessity, to partnerships. Well before bombs fell upon Pearl Harbor, Japan was formally aligned with Germany. In certain geopolitical ways having to do with global domination, the alliance made sense. In others, it seemed unnatural. The Japanese were clasped in an embrace with a Reich that preached the superiority—the inevitable ascension—of the Aryan race. But as the 1940s loomed, the world's nations were not choosing sides strictly on the basis of philosophy. Equally relevant questions were: How can I best survive? What's in it for me? And, of course, Who's knocking at the door?

Mainichi Newspaper/Pana

Underwood Photo Archives

The warrior ethos was deeply ingrained in Japan well before the 20th century, with ancient traditions exalting the samurai. The purity of the nobleman's code of combat was diluted in the late 1800s when modernized armies blended Western weaponry and technology with Japanese principles of courage, fierceness and a willingness to fight to the death. Some lamented the dilution of the samurai philosophy, but Japan's new hybrid war machine was extremely effective. In 1905 it defeated Russia in a war for Manchuria and Korea, and within five years was showing might on the seas in armored ships. Japan had sided with the Allies in the First World War, but when Britain and France redrew boundaries in Europe and Asia, Japan was upset by the limits of its new dominion. Beginning in the early 1920s, the island nation began flexing its muscle, spending large amounts of money in an attempt to build the world's largest naval air force.

In 1931 the empire launched its undeclared war on China's heartland by extending its reach in Manchuria, which it renamed Manchukuo. Chinese soldiers, debilitated by the war between Mao Zedong's communists and Chiang Kai-shek's Nationalists, were unable to resist as, throughout the decade, Japan pushed south through Beijing and on toward Shanghai. Four qualities invariably marked the Japanese attack: efficiency, discipline, brutality and, especially, surprise. John Paul Jones once observed, "Whoever can surprise well must

Japanese schoolchildren practiced signaling (top), and marines headed into battle in Shanghai (right). After that city fell in November 1937, Japan attacked and took the Chinese capital at Nanjing. An orgy of rape and murder ensued. "[W]e pushed [the Chinese] into the ditch, and had their hairs lighted so as to see them lingering to die," boasted one soldier.

from

es of

9840

85

In 1937, a crying infant was all that seemed to survive a Japanese air raid on Shanghai's South Railway Station. Shanghai, China's most important industrial and business center and the site of its largest port, was especially coveted by Tokyo. The last remaining Western-controlled sectors were taken by Japan on December 8, 1941—even as it attacked Pearl Harbor.

conquer." The spirit of this maxim informed everything that Japan did militarily up to, and certainly including, Pearl Harbor.

In the years leading to 1941, Japan's intentions were to dominate China and then expand its empire where it might. Initial targets beyond Manchuria included the eastern Chinese cities and Mongolia, but it soon became evident that Japan needed additional resources to fuel its burgeoning campaign. New targets were chosen, including mineral-rich Indochina and oil-rich Indonesia, colonies of France and Holland. With the 1940 German victories over the European mother countries, these Pacific outposts seemed ripe for picking.

In the summer of that year, the Japanese government, which was dominated by militarists—most prominently, War Minister Tojo Hideki, a man described as "the fiercest hawk in the Orient"—decided that the future should include an alliance with Germany, an effort to resume trade with the U.S. (which had been halted by Washington to protest Japan's incursions in China and elsewhere in the Far East) and an offensive in Southeast Asia. As dealmakers flew to Europe and negotiators to America, fighter planes and bombers were readied for sorties in the Pacific.

Tensions between the U.S. and Japan over China continued to worsen. Early in the new year, on January 7, 1941, Adm. Yamamoto Isoroku, Commander in Chief of Japan's Combined Fleet, offered his "Views on Preparations for War." The plans included a strategy that stunned most of his colleagues and confirmed the appraisal of one of them, that Yamamoto had "a gambler's heart." The big wager in Yamamoto's "Views" was that a surprise attack on the U.S. fleet at Pearl Harbor could result in a quick victory, which would prompt the U.S. to petition for peace in the Pacific. Yamamoto never anticipated a

Hirohito showed his distaste for his government's saber-rattling by expressing the hope that the next prime minister would be "one who has no fascist leanings, and about whom there has been no unsavory rumor, who is moderate in thought and who is not militaristic."

The Son of Heaven

Hirohito was born in 1901 in Tokyo, and despite the obvious amenities, life for the young crown prince was often bleak and lonely. On those rare occasions when he was permitted to play with other children, he proved clumsy: Hirohito was extremely nearsighted, but in his culture, gods had no need for eyeglasses. There were some better times. He became the first Japanese crown prince to travel abroad when, at the age of 19, he spent six delightful, liberating months in Europe.

Hirohito ascended the Chrysanthemum Throne on December 25, 1926, following the death of his father. Japan at the time was becoming increasingly democratic and internationalist; by the early 1930s, however, a martial influence had swept the country. Some accounts maintain that the emperor was unsympathetic, opposed to both the alliance with Germany and Italy and the prospect of war with the U.S. Other historians contend, though, that Hirohito was all along complicit with Japanese expansionist policies. What is clear is that, near the war's end, Hirohito sided with those who sought peace rather than those who wanted to fight to the death. Several of his advisers were tried and convicted of war crimes, but not the emperor.

In 1946, Hirohito renounced any claims to divinity. In his later years he made frequent public appearances in an effort to reach out to commoners. The man himself was doubtless happiest when indulging his lifelong interest in marine-biology research, publishing several well-received volumes on his specialty, the jellyfish.

The Showa Emperor died in 1989. It was a name he had long ago chosen for his reign. "Showa" means Enlightened Peace.

surrender—he wasn't seeking one, nor did he feel that Japan would necessarily prevail in a drawn-out war with America—but rather a settlement that would allow Japan to pursue its prospecting in Sumatra, Borneo, Java and French Indochina.

Within three weeks of Yamamoto's presentation, U.S. Ambassador to Japan Joseph C. Grew heard a disquieting rumor. He cabled Washington: "My Peruvian colleague told a member of my staff that he had heard from many sources including a Japanese source that the Japanese military forces planned, in the event of trouble with the United States, to attempt a surprise mass attack on Pearl Harbor using all their military facilities." Warnings about

Pearl Harbor's vulnerability were nothing new. As long before as 1924, Brig. Gen. Billy Mitchell, then assistant chief of the Army Air Service, had returned from an inspection tour to report that Pacific defenses were inadequate, and even to predict that, if the Japanese were to attack Oahu, they would do well to begin with Ford Island at 7:30 in the morning. A January 1938 U.S. War Department survey of Pearl Harbor's defenses had said that if the Japanese attacked, they would do so without notice, and "there can be little doubt that the Hawaiian Islands will be the initial scene of action." On January 24, 1941, three days before Grew reported his rumor, Navy Secretary Frank Knox mailed a letter to the

In October 1940 in Tokyo, Tojo (center, in boots), along with German and Italian representatives, toasted the signing of the Axis alliance. The pact made the Japanese willing conspirators in a war that would claim 60 million lives.

Emperor Hirohito led an inspection tour in Osaka of giant listening horns intended to pick up the sound of approaching enemy aircraft. The horns exemplify not only Japan's constant search for the next big technological idea but also the extent of the country's xenophobia in the 1930s.

Illustration/Keystone/Gamma

command at Pearl Harbor that said a reexamination of the base's readiness had been undertaken, "prompted by the increased gravity of the situation with respect to Japan, and by reports from abroad of successful bombing and torpedo plane attacks on ships while in bases."

The conclusions of the reappraisal were, said Knox: "If war eventuates with Japan, it is believed easily possible that hostilities would be initiated by a surprise attack upon the Fleet or the Naval Base at Pearl Harbor. In my opinion, the inherent possibilities of a major disaster to the Fleet or Naval Base warrant taking every step, as rapidly as can be done, that will increase the joint readiness of the Army and Navy to withstand a raid of the character mentioned above."

Every step was not taken, of course, as the information supplied by both Knox and Grew—and Mitchell well before them—was largely ignored in Washington.

And perhaps that was understandable, since nothing about any surprise attack was turning up in the MAGIC transcripts.

In August 1940, Lt. Col. William F. Friedman of the Army Signal Corps had succeeded in cracking the complex Japanese diplomatic code called PURPLE, and quickly a series of machines, also called PURPLE, had been built and put into action. They translated intercepts of Japanese transmissions between Tokyo and its emissaries in Washington, and the messages, called MAGIC by the Americans, were then circulated among U.S. officials. The U.S. knew about Japan's designs on Southeast Asia but learned nothing from PURPLE about Pearl Harbor. Just so: Throughout 1941, information about the daring assault was so closely held by officials in Tokyo that they apparently kept even their ambassador to the U.S., Nomura Kichisaburo, in the dark.

Japan was not, of course, just a war machine; it

In March 1941, kids in Osaka took part in an air-raid drill (above), as adults had done in the same city the previous September (below). The precautions would prove prudent when, on April 18, 1942, Lt. Col. Jimmy Doolittle led the first Allied air raid on Tokyo.

was a society as well. It had an emperor. He was a still-young man named Hirohito, who had taken the throne in 1926 at age 25.

He was, essentially, an onlooker to his country's aggression. Out of deference to an ancient system, generals and government officials routinely made presentations to the emperor, but these were hardly consultations. Hirohito and some moderate politicians occasionally issued calls for peace throughout the 1930s and into the '40s. But the emperor was politely ignored by the militarists, and the pols were, one by one, replaced. Civilian government was eroding in Japan, as censorship and propaganda routed any temperate views. The generals succeeded in inflaming a national xenophobia and sense of righteousness.

The last chapter of Japan's march to world war began at one of Hirohito's Imperial Conferences, this one held on September 6, 1941. There, the cabinet officially adopted the military's war plan. The emperor, in turn, read a poem written by his grandfather: "In a world/ Where all the seas/ Are brethren,/ Why do wind and wave/ So stridently clash?" A lingering moderate in the government, Prince Konoye Fumimaro, Japan's premier, sensed that the emperor's mindset might point to an escape from disaster. In a meeting that evening with Ambassador Grew, Konoye requested an audience with President Roosevelt to see whether a peaceful solution could be

Students huddled at a bomb shelter in Osaka during a drill in October 1941. U.S. air raids would not strike the Japanese mainland with regularity for another three years but by war's end would kill or wound nearly a million.

reached. As Grew took the request to Washington, Konoye asked Yamamoto whether his navy was prepared, should the overture be rebuffed. "If you insist on my going ahead," the admiral replied, "I can promise to give them hell for a year or a year and a half, but can guarantee nothing as to what will happen after that." Yamamoto had been to the U.S. and was worried that the industrial machine there, coupled with the stores of fuel in Texas oil fields, would eventually overwhelm any foe.

Roosevelt, counseled by Secretary of State Cordell Hull, who of course knew of Japan's constant duplicity through the MAGIC dispatches, told the Japanese that summits were pointless without Japanese capitulation on China (and now French Indochina, which Japan had brazenly occupied in midsummer).

On October 16, Konoye resigned as premier. He was succeeded by Tojo, who the previous year had been made Minister of War. Soon after, Adm. Nagano Osami approved Yamamoto's Pearl Harbor plan, and a week after that Tojo addressed a meeting of 200 government officials: "We must go on to develop in ever-expanding progression. There is no retreat." On November 17, Yamamoto gave a similar speech to key members of the First Air Fleet aboard the flagship *Akagi*: "Although we hope to achieve surprise, everyone should be prepared for terrific American resistance in this operation." A toast was raised to success in the coming battle: "Banzai! Banzai! Banzai!"

The opening of an armor-plate factory in Philadelphia in mid-1941 led to this patriotic display. The plant was owned by Henry Disston and Sons, whose usual business was making handsaws.

Corbis-Bettmann

In 1941, a majority of Americans, while sympathetic to the foreign oppressed, reserved their energies for matters close to home. Precious jobs had to be found or maintained, precious food harvested or scrounged. In a nation emerging from the brutal Depression, few citizens wanted any part of another debilitating fight. Extreme isolationists wouldn't even pick sides; most Americans allowed that you could tell good guys from bad and that the U.S. should back the democracies however it could— short of sending our boys. In Washington, President Roosevelt took the public's pulse but also saw where things were headed. He ordered buildup after buildup of arms and men. As November turned to December, he felt that something was about to give.

Members of the Massachusetts Women's Political Club paid a visit to the White House on February 25, 1941, to present a petition decrying the Lend-lease Agreement. That the Depression, and even World War I, weren't far removed from the public mind was never lost on FDR. The President contended, however, that "the best immediate defense of the United States is the success of Great Britain defending itself."

Prior to December 7, 1941, there was an overarching difference between the United States and its foes, Germany, Italy and Japan. They were already at war, and America wasn't. Yes, there was a sense of emergency, something akin to the feeling of wartime, in America: A billion-and-a-half-dollar increase to upgrade the Army and build more planes in May 1940 was followed by another billion for the Army later that year, plus nearly $700 million for the Navy. On September 16, the first U.S. peacetime draft was instituted. But for all of this building up and battening down, the Neutrality Act, which had been made law by a country that wanted, after its experience in World War I, to stay off the battlefield at all costs, still obtained. Roosevelt could chip away at neutrality and isolationism as much as he wanted with words—words informed by a keen appreciation of where Hitler and Tojo were headed—but he couldn't make his countrymen go to war if they weren't ready to go.

And they wouldn't be ready until their hand was forced. If massive increases in defense spending and armament manufacture told one tale, the polls told another. A survey taken immediately after the 1939 outbreak of war in Europe showed that 30 percent of Americans were still dedicated to complete neutrality and an embargo on all belligerents, while 37 percent favored neutrality with trade allowed on a cash-and-carry basis. Add it up, and you get two thirds of the U.S. still in favor of neutrality. By June 1940, just after Italy declared war, 67 percent of the nation were in favor of aiding the Allies, but only 27 percent were prepared to go to war. A month later this number had fallen to 15 percent. To secure reelection to a historic third term in 1940, Roosevelt ran on a plank that promised to keep America out of the war. Even as comic-strip hero Joe Palooka was urging his manager Knobby Walsh

Brown Brothers

Last-Ditch Efforts

In the nine months leading to Bloody Sunday, Secretary of State **Cordell Hull** met 40 times with Japanese ambassador **Nomura Kichisaburo.** The two men failed, of course, to prevent war, but their talks have long been grist for historians.

Hull's reputation—built over 11 years and nine months on the job, then topped with the Nobel Peace Prize in 1945—is that of a peacemaker who was clear-eyed about war. In the 1930s, he scored a resounding success with his Good Neighbor Policy in Latin America, and his diplomacy fostered a united front of American countries against the Axis. Regarding Japan, his record is less certain. Some historians credit him with great patience as he tried to strengthen the position of Japanese moderates. Others maintain that Hull's penchant for sermonizing and ceaseless deliberation ultimately served him poorly in the attempt to avoid war in the Pacific.

Concerning Nomura, the question is whether he bargained in good faith: Did he know about the planned sneak attack? In all probability, he did not. He certainly made a good overall impression on Hull during negotiations, and the historical

consensus seems to be that Nomura was a decent, honorable man. Knowing him to be such, the Imperial Navy probably wouldn't have trusted him to carry out a critical deception. Also: Why would Nomura be in a "need to know" position?

In the event, it didn't matter. On December 7, Hull excoriated Nomura for his deceit, and the image of the treacherous ambassador was firmly lodged in America's wartime craw.

Secretary of State Hull escorted Ambassador Nomura (left) and special envoy Kurusu Saburo to the White House on November 17, 1941.

During a worldwide broadcast on May 27, 1941, FDR proclaimed "that an unlimited national emergency confronts this country, which requires that its military, naval, air and civilian defenses [be readied] to repel any and all acts or threats of aggression." Sen. Burton Wheeler replied that Roosevelt was "preaching fear."

to spend $10,000 on savings bonds instead of a race horse, an October 1941 Gallup Poll showed that a majority of Americans had no intention to buy savings bonds or stamps. At the same time, a poll by *Fortune* magazine found that people were concerned that the future would bring higher prices, fewer jobs and fewer opportunities for their children. These were the big issues.

So the United States was living two lives: The political, which saw entry into the world war, in some fashion, as an inevitability. And the day-to-day, which fully realized there was a threat but dared to hope that war could be avoided.

The man straddling the gulf was Roosevelt. He was by no means a hawk, but he was a realist, and he was receiving real information each day not only from his generals but also from Secretary of State Cordell Hull, a smart and tough man open to negotiation when it might bear fruit but ready to resort to other means when talking proved fruitless. Roosevelt and Hull knew they were dealing

with a public that generally didn't want to fight, and that included a strong minority—a minority that would remain vocal through December 6, 1941—that wanted America to stay out of war, come what may.

Very few isolationists sided with the Nazis, and there was no thinking that Japan should rule China. But most isolationists believed that the wars in Europe and Asia were not their country's affair. Europe was an old, always warring place—a place that Americans had left. Moreover, battered by the Depression, Americans were having no easy time propping up their own nation. The United States should not get involved in the tribal feuds of ancestors (went the reasoning). And it could not—not at that moment. Furthermore, citizens and generals had all seen how the U.S. pitched in at the eleventh hour to help Britain and France win the Great War only to find American recommendations at Versailles snubbed. Would the Yanks bail them out again, at blood cost, and again get nothing in return?

Lindbergh inspected an airplane plant in Bremen, Germany, in 1936 (above), and spoke at an America First rally (left) in Chicago in April 1941. A week later, columnist-with-clout Walter Winchell said of a similar gathering: "More American flags than Americans."

These arguments seemed reasonable throughout the 1930s and eventually coalesced into formal associations. The Committee to Defend America by Aiding the Allies said that the U.S. should remain neutral but assist Great Britain: A British victory would keep the world a stable place, safe for democracies. This sounded like double-speak to the America First Committee, which insisted that it was more important to stay out of the war than to try to back either horse.

America Firsters grew to be 800,000 in number. One among them was transcendentally famous and influential. This was Charles A. Lindbergh, the great hero of the air. His popularity in America since his solo flight across the Atlantic in 1927 had never waned; if anything, it had increased after the 1932 kidnapping and murder of his first son. He was a celebrity of the highest magnitude. Lucky Lindy was a national institution.

Then, after several visits to Nazi Germany, Lucky

Lindy told his countrymen that intervention was not only wrong from a philosophical standpoint but unwise from a military one. The Luftwaffe is one strong flying machine, Lindbergh reported, and the Germans really know how to get things done.

Lindbergh was not necessarily a Nazi sympathizer, but he was a man of firm opinions and, throughout the 1930s and into the '40s, a man of mistakes. On one visit to Germany, he attended a stag dinner hosted by Hitler henchman Hermann Goering, and during the festivities Lindbergh accepted a medal. Later that night he showed it to his wife, Anne Morrow Lindbergh, who saw it for what it would become, and said quietly, "the albatross."

Remaining polite while accepting a medal might have been explained away, but the Des Moines speech could not be. There, in September 1941, Lindbergh spoke the words—words his wife warned him not to utter—that reflected a philosophy that would forever tarnish his image and would, in the near term, soil the America First movement. Addressing a crowd of like thinkers, Lindbergh proclaimed that the British government, the Roosevelt administration and "the Jews" were spoiling for intervention—and he could understand that, since it was their constituencies at risk—but that Americans should see these "war agitators" for what they were, and oppose them.

This was a problem. Are we not all Americans? asked many of Lindbergh's countrymen. And, of course, the bit about the Jews smacked of anti-Semitism, which in 1941 was a very short leap from Nazism. With the possibility of war looming larger every day, Lindbergh had laid himself—and his movement—open to fierce criticism. Roosevelt publicly denounced him. Lindbergh countered by resigning his commission in the Army Air Corps Reserve. (Only weeks later, with Pearl Harbor smoldering, he would try to reenlist but would be turned down.)

If isolationists came in several stripes and degrees of intensity, and were inspired in their cause by everything from abject fear to racial bigotry, then those who admitted to being interventionists came in one kind only. They saw Hitler's march as an evil thing—a totalitarian purge of Europe's free societies. They worried that it might become an effort at world domination. Because the Japanese were in league with the Germans, they were part of the equation, the product of which

could be a world controlled by Hitler (and maybe Mussolini) in the West, Tojo in the East.

But intervention equated, from day one, with American death—and so it was insupportable to most.

Thus was the country split, with the majority favoring an opposition to Hitler, a measured support of European democracies and every effort to not send our boys to the battlefield. On December 7 this massive part of the populace, having been primed over time by Roosevelt, would shout out loud: Let's go get 'em. Or, as Sen. Burton K. Wheeler, who awoke that day a fervent isolationist, put it: "The only thing now to do is to lick hell out of them."

War Secretary Henry Stimson began the first U.S. peacetime draft while blindfolded with a swatch taken from the chair used by signers of the Declaration of Independence. By the end of 1940, many a mom and sis had wished "Godspeed!"

They were stressful times, but for indispensables like baseball and romance, there was always room. In late September this Brooklyn bar was ripe for revelry as patrons celebrated the National League pennant their Dodgers had just brought home. Only days later, "King of Swing" Benny Goodman chatted with a sailor and his amour in the Hotel New Yorker's Terrace Room. They requested their favorite tune, *You and I.*

Culver Pictures

So how did this interesting political situation impact the day-to-day?

Greatly, and in graphic ways. In America in 1941, fear had purchase, and fatalism, sometimes manifested as a let's-dance-while-we-can denial, was in the air.

"Two-fifths of our people are more interested in the baseball scores than they are in foreign news," wrote William Allen White in the *Emporia Gazette* as the summer wound down. And why not? Joe DiMaggio had hit in 56 straight games that magical season, and Ted Williams had batted .406. Joe Louis, heavyweight champ since 1938, whomped seven more members of the Bum of the Month Club in 1941.

Many Americans were reading William L. Shirer's *Berlin Diary.* Many others were reading F. Scott Fitzgerald's posthumously published novel of Hollywood, *The Last Tycoon.* In New York City, Glenn Miller, Benny Goodman, Duke Ellington,

Harry James and Guy Lombardo ruled the clubs and ballrooms. Helen Hayes, Ethel Barrymore, Gertrude Lawrence and Danny Kaye were on Broadway in shows by Noel Coward, Lillian Hellman and Cole Porter.

Upstate in the Adirondacks, skiers were practicing for possible military action in Europe. Down in Georgia, vocational schools were teaching young people to build ships, planes and guns. Out in Los Angeles, 6,000 artillerymen were working with their antiaircraft weapons, getting ready for an air-raid drill. In Chicago, paperboys tried to sell war stamps door-to-door.

In the papers during the first week of December, an ad for a sunlamp boosted the benefits of ultraviolet rays, and another said that a carton of cigarettes would make the perfect Christmas gift. Yet another poll indicated that 58 percent of Americans didn't exercise apart from their jobs. *The Boston Globe* had a recommendation for young

George Strock

parents: "Do not punish your child by not allowing him to have his ice cream. Ice cream is a good food and is valuable for both energy and body building." Another *Globe* article had tips for wives: "DON'T serve him scrambled newspapers instead of scrambled eggs for breakfast. DON'T make a sad and I-don't-understand-it face when he laughs his head off over 'the best joke of the century.'"

On Cape Cod, 23,000 new troops arrived at Camp Edwards while taps sounded in the background. At Filene's, you couldn't get proper stockings because of the embargo on Japanese silk. A Boston hairdresser was using cotton thread instead of metal bobby pins to keep a 'do in place.

Anne Morrow Lindbergh, who would eventually say that her husband had been used by the Nazis, wrote that week: "Soldiers on the train, searchlights in the sky, planes maneuvering in threes. All the billboards have gone 'Defense' mad, with pictures of soldiers and sailors on them. *Vogue* photographs its

Soldiers' morale skyrocketed when Hollywood lovelies led the cheers. Right: Dorothy Lamour was the Army's favorite pinup girl when she dined, in July 1941, with these soldiers in Honolulu. Her remarkable fund-raising efforts would earn her the sobriquet Bond Bombshell. Below: a young Jane Russell at the Army Air Corps's advanced flying school on July 11, 1941.

models in front of Bundles for Britain planes. Longchamps has V's done in vegetables in the windows. Elizabeth Arden gets out a V for Victory lipstick."

In magazine ads that first week of December, General Motors would have Americans believe "Defense Comes First with Oldsmobile!" and Remington asserted, "Victory Begins at a Thousand Peaceful Desks."

You could escape the war imagery. At the movies, *Dr. Jekyll and Mr. Hyde, Here Comes Mr. Jordan, The Maltese Falcon* and *Dumbo* were playing. (On the evening of December 6, however, no one in several cities could see *Two-Faced Woman,* in which Greta Garbo played twin sisters sleeping with the same man. The Catholic Legion of Decency had earlier won its battle to have the film withdrawn.)

In the nation's capital, Hull learned, from intercepted messages, that Japan had set a firm deadline of November 29 to put its operations into motion. The American government knew, in this first week of December, that something was coming.

LIFE ran a story that week on the Japanese diplomatic efforts, profiling emissaries Kurusu Saburo and Nomura Kichisaburo in an article

headlined, JAPANESE BOW AND GRIN FOR THE CAMERA BUT GET NOWHERE IN WASHINGTON.

Secretary of the Navy Frank Knox released his annual report on December 6, which read in part, "the American people may feel fully confident in their Navy. In my opinion, the loyalty, morale and technical ability of the personnel are without superior. On any comparable basis, the United States Navy is second to none."

Another poll: The week before Pearl Harbor, according to Gallup, 52 percent of Americans thought the U.S. would go to war against Japan "sometime in the near future." A December 7 headline in *The New York Times*—JAPAN RATTLES SWORD BUT ECHO IS PIANISSIMO—was belied by an eerie sense of foreboding that, finally, had touched a majority of Americans. Better to rely not on journalism that weekend but on the horoscope, which predicted "strange, sudden and wholly unpredictable and inexplicable occurrences affecting all phases of life."

In Honolulu on Saturday, officers played golf at the Fort Shafter course. Twenty-four thousand football fans watched the University of Hawaii Rainbows beat Willamette. After nightfall, sailors cruised Hotel Street, and some of them took in the floor show with the "Tantalizing Tootsies" at the Princess. Elsewhere, there was a dinner at the Pearl Harbor Officers' Club, and a battle of the fleet's dance bands. The swinging outfit from the *Pennsylvania* won. All members of the *Arizona*'s band would die the next day.

On the night of December 6, Lt. Gen. Walter C. Short, commander of the U.S. Army's Hawaiian Department, gazed upon the harbor. He noted the twinkling lights of the battleships and observed, "Isn't that a beautiful sight? And what a target they would make."

Hula dancers performed for sailors aboard the USS *Honolulu* in July 1939. A month earlier the light cruiser had been made the flagship of Rear Adm. Husband E. Kimmel. The *Honolulu* would be damaged but not sunk in the attack on Pearl Harbor. Above: The Black Cat Cafe was a favorite haven for servicemen.

These snapshots were taken in Hawaii from 1939 to 1941. The sailor at top left was belowdecks on the *Arizona*. The soldier being cradled by his buddies at top right is Sgt. Robert Waltermire, who was the longtime staff driver of Gen. Walter C. Short.

A gaggle of gobs strolled Waikiki Beach, a popular destination for servicemen on leave. Right: With Diamond Head providing a dynamic backdrop, these sailors enjoyed the prewar waves of Waikiki.

These photos from September 1941 show the seven Patten brothers, who served together on the *Nevada*. At top and right, the lads pursued traditional shipboard activities. Above: Following his enlistment in the Navy, father Clarence was hoisted by Myrne, Ray, Allen, Bruce, Gilbert, Marvin and Clarence Jr. All survived the attack.

Right: In the fall of 1941, this all-Marine whaleboat team from the *Arizona* took second place in the Pacific Fleet competition. Only two of the men survived the attack: Sgt. John McRay Baker (in T-shirt) and Pvt. Russell J. McCurdy (bottom row, far right). Below: There were 21 men in Unit Band 22, attached to the *Arizona*. All would perish at the band's battle station as they were attempting to pass ammunition under Turrets No. 1 and 2.

USS Arizona Memorial/NPS (2)

The annual Christmas lights on Fort Street in Honolulu provided a merry setting. It was only days before the attack on Pearl Harbor would shut down the display, and put an end to seasonal cheer.

4 DECEMBER 7, 1941

Admiral Yamamoto called the U.S. fleet at Pearl Harbor "a dagger pointed at our throat." Secretary of State Hull's opinion of Japanese aggression had distilled to: "Nothing will stop them but force." Yamamoto's attack was put in motion as Japanese aircraft carriers moved across the Pacific, closing the 3,400 miles between Japan and Hawaii. President Roosevelt could only sit and wait, having determined that the blow that would force America to arms would come from Japan—not Germany—and that the U.S. must let the blow land rather than issue a first strike. The eve of the bombing was an eerie calm before the storm as, for politicians if not for the public, war had already become a reality. The duel was engaged, with guns yet to be fired.

U.S. Navy

I n the last week of November, Japan's deadline to put its attack plan in motion finally arrived. Vice Admiral Nagumo Chuichi assembled the staffs of his carriers, battleships, cruisers, destroyers and submarines, and for the first time revealed to them that their target was Pearl Harbor. They had three days to digest the news; then ships and planes started making their way east-southeast. Nagumo and his fleet had already been at sea for more than 24 hours when, in Washington, Secretary of State Hull met with Japanese diplomats Nomura Kichisaburo and Kurusu Saburo, who were, it seemed, unaware of the mobilization and the attack plans in general. Hull wanted to discuss America's Ten Points, which amounted to a renewed demand for Japan's withdrawal from China and Indochina as a principal condition for any negotiated peace. Nomura and Kurusu treated the discussions with due seriousness, but if Hull needed confirmation that the talks were largely worthless, he got it on November 29 when he received a copy of a speech Tojo had just given in Japan. While short of a formal declaration of war, the speech was certainly intended to inspire the Japanese military. Hull called Roosevelt, who was vacationing in Warm Springs, Ga., and, as he later recalled, impressed upon the President "the imminent danger of a Japanese attack, and advised him to advance the date of his return to Washington." Roosevelt packed his bags.

USS Arizona Memorial/NPS (2)

This banquet on the carrier *Akagi* on November 25, 1941, celebrated the grand mission that lay ahead. Commander Fuchida Mitsuo, who would lead the air attack, is seated at rear, third from right. Inset: A toast was raised on the *Akagi*. Top left: Vice Admiral Nagumo Chuichi, Commander in Chief of the First Air Fleet. From the beginning, he was adamant that Yamamoto's plan was riddled with problems.

Did Roosevelt Know?

The attack on Pearl Harbor is one of the most odious chapters in American history. And of the many questions raised therein, the most unappetizing is one that is heard increasingly: Did **President Franklin Delano Roosevelt** know ahead of time where and when the attack would come?

It is clear that Roosevelt, more than most of his countrymen, recognized early on that Americans would not be able to isolate themselves from the conflict that would become known as World War II. His repeated calls for increased military readiness and for measures such as the Lend-lease pact show that he considered war to be unavoidable. Such prescience, however, reflects access to classified information rather than any personal desire to enter into an unnecessary fight.

One weapon frequently wielded by revisionists is the fact that, because the U.S. had broken the Japanese PURPLE code long before Pearl Harbor, military intelligence had access to messages that must have alerted them to specific Japanese intentions. Indeed, the intelligence gathering was remarkable, but intelligence that is passed on improperly, ineffectually—or simply not picked up on—is often worse than none whatsoever. It's entirely possible that had the code not been broken, American preparedness would have been better.

President Roosevelt and Cordell Hull shared a ride to the White House on August 17, 1941. FDR had just returned from his historic meeting at sea with Churchill.

It has been six decades since the attack—60 years for countless historians to pore over the material at hand. It is not enough to refer to messages that no longer exist, to rely on hearsay about someone's mood before bedtime on December 6. After all these years, it comes down to this: No smoking gun has been found.

Furthermore, why would the President have risked the destruction of his beloved Pacific Fleet at the onset of a global confrontation? Surely there were better ways to pick a fight.

On December 1, Japanese land forces swept south through Indochina, while Nagumo's ocean-going task force was now halfway to Hawaii, having crossed the international date line unnoticed. One of Nagumo's aides later remembered the 12-day sail across a "vacant sea" as "the most difficult and most agonizing period for every officer in the Naval General Staff who knew about Pearl Harbor."

While the ships made their quiet way across the Pacific, Japan was in action throughout the globe. In Washington, the Japanese negotiators were trying to keep their American counterparts engaged, promising that an answer to the Ten Points would be forthcoming. In Germany, another ambassador, Oshima Hiroshi, was huddling with Nazi foreign minister Joachim von Ribbentrop, letting the Axis partners know that there existed "extreme danger

that war may suddenly break out between the Anglo-Saxon nations and Japan through some clash of arms … this war may come quicker than anyone dreams." Ribbentrop assured Oshima, "Should Japan become engaged in a war against the United States, Germany, of course, would join the war immediately. There is absolutely no possibility of Germany's entering into a separate peace with the United States under such circumstances. The Führer is determined on that point."

In Tokyo on December 1, another Imperial Conference was held at Hirohito's palace. After plans were reviewed and Tojo made an impassioned speech, the emperor nodded his head, thereby giving his consent to all-out war. "His Majesty," wrote an observer, "seemed to be in an excellent mood, and we were filled with awe." Later that day, about

It is ironic that Yamamoto Isoroku, the grand master of the attack plan, was perhaps the one man in Japan who most feared war with the U.S. In April 1943, Intelligence learned that he was flying to Bougainville island in the Pacific, and he was shot down by American P-38s.

AP/Wide World

Archive Photos

Photographed from the flagship *Akagi,* the aircraft carrier *Kaga* (above) steamed through heavy seas en route to Pearl Harbor. With typical naval superstition, Japanese sailors regarded the *Kaga* as a "victorious" ship because she had enjoyed success off of China in the 1930s. The carrier *Zuikaku* is visible at right. Admiral Nagumo (below, center) stood on the bridge of the *Akagi* as it made for Hawaii.

940 miles north of the Midway islands, Nagumo received Yamamoto's message to proceed: "Climb Mount Niitaka, 1208." The number referred to the eighth day of the 12th month, which on the Hawaiian side of the international date line would be December 7, 1941.

On December 2 at Pearl Harbor, Adm. Husband E. Kimmel, head of the Navy command, discussed intelligence reports with his aide. He asked Lt. Cdr. Edwin T. Layton for updates on the location of Japan's aircraft carriers. Layton gave estimates for all except the four carriers in Divisions 1 and 2. "What!" Kimmel said. "You don't know where Carrier Division 1 and Carrier Division 2 are?"

"No, sir, I do not," replied Layton. "I think they are in home waters but I do not know where they are. The rest of these units, I feel pretty confident of their locations."

"Do you mean to say," challenged Kimmel, "that they could be rounding Diamond Head and you wouldn't know it?"

"I hope they would be sighted before now," said Layton.

The next day—Wednesday, December 3—two Japanese communications were intercepted and translated into MAGIC memorandums. The first, already more than two weeks old, directed the Japanese consulate in Honolulu to step up its periodic reports on the location of American warships in Pearl Harbor. The message was seen as not especially important because the Japanese had long been attempting reconnaissances of American naval bases. The second intercept was a reply from Tojo to his ambassadors, who had suggested that war might be averted through a summit conference at "some midway point, such as Honolulu." Tojo's answer: "[I]t would be inappropriate for us to propose such a meeting."

Roosevelt tried one last time to petition for peace. On December 6, he drafted a personal appeal to Hirohito and had it encoded and sent, at approximately 9 p.m., to Ambassador Grew in Tokyo. At just about that time, Ambassador Nomura received word in Washington that an answer to the Ten Points was coming immediately in the form of a 14-part memo. In late afternoon and early evening, the first 13 parts of the memo were intercepted, deciphered and sent to Roosevelt. When the President finished reading the items, which included nothing helpful—mostly threats—he said, "This means war."

The 14th part of the Japanese message was not received and circulated in Washington until the morning of December 7, and at that point a follow-up memorandum was also intercepted. Part 14 stated that Japan was terminating diplomatic relations with the U.S., and the postscript instructed Ambassador Nomura to deliver the Japanese view to Cordell Hull at 1 o'clock. Realizing that 1 p.m. on the East Coast corresponded to daybreak in the Pacific, intelligence officer Col. Rufus S. Bratton hurriedly sought to warn his superiors of a possible attack. A message was drafted and sent to commanders in California, Panama, the Philippines and Hawaii: "The Japanese are presenting at 1 p.m. E.S.T. today what amounts to an ultimatum, also they are under orders to destroy their code machine immediately. Just what significance the hour set may have we do not know but be on alert accordingly."

By 12:01 p.m. on the East Coast—6:31 a.m. in

On Their Watch

With any disaster, particularly one as notorious as Pearl Harbor, there is a rush to judgment. How could it have happened? Who is responsible?

Official investigations began at once with a board of inquiry appointed by President Roosevelt and chaired by Supreme Court Justice Owen J. Roberts. On January 23, 1942, the Roberts Commission found that **Adm. Husband E. Kimmel** (right), Commander in Chief of the Pacific Fleet, and **Lt. Gen. Walter C. Short** (below), commanding officer of the Army's Hawaiian Department, were

guilty of "dereliction of duty" and "errors of judgment [that] were the effective causes for the success of the attack." Kimmel and Short, who had already been relieved of their commands, retired shortly after Roberts's report was issued.

A half dozen military tribunals were conducted before the war's end, but none had access to all the evidence. Immediately after the war, a congressional investigation was begun; the hearings inspired the same

sort of public fascination as Teapot Dome had or Watergate would. Criticism fell upon many, and Kimmel and Short were cleared of dereliction of duty, but they were still blamed for shortcomings. The complete exoneration that the two friends had fought so bitterly for eluded them. Ever since, both men have had staunch supporters who have worked tirelessly to restore their reputations. Indeed, as recently as May 25, 1999, the Senate voted to exonerate them posthumously, but President Clinton declined to sign the measure into law.

The debate all along has turned on what information the two officers had from Washington, and how they acted on it. There were warnings on November 27 and earlier, but a warning about war doesn't constitute a warning about an attack. On the other hand, officials in Washington couldn't advise of a Japanese action that they themselves could not accurately predict.

Kimmel and Short are in many ways sympathetic figures. When a fiasco like Pearl Harbor comes along, however, the buck has to stop somewhere. In this case, it stopped with the men who, for whatever reasons, failed to cope with the attack.

December 7: Fuchida Mitsuo (above) told Nagumo, "I am ready for the mission." The admiral said, "I have every confidence in you." And the attack commenced. Left: Crewmen cheered as a bomber departed.

Hawaii—the warning was filed at the War Department Signal Center for transmission to Panama, Manila and San Francisco. The War Department had been out of contact with Hawaii that morning and was attempting to relay the message to Honolulu; Teletype transmission to San Francisco was completed by 12:17 p.m. Washington time (6:47 a.m. in Hawaii). The warning was sent from San Francisco to RCA's Honolulu office, where it arrived at 7:33 a.m. Because that was too early for Teletype traffic to Fort Shafter, RCA sent the memo by messenger: a Japanese boy on a motorcycle. En route, the boy heard what sounded like gunfire.

Several minutes earlier, elsewhere on Oahu, two trainees had been preparing to close down the radar for daylight hours when they noticed blips on the screen—planes approaching at a range of 132 miles. Their lieutenant was not surprised; a flight of Fortresses from the West Coast was expected. Shut it down, he suggested, and go get some chow.

The strike force for Japan's Hawaiian Operation had begun to assemble at Hitokappu Bay in the Kuril Islands in November, while elsewhere, Japanese army and air corps units prepared to sweep other Pacific islands during, or right after, the assault on Pearl Harbor. By month's end, Japan wanted to lock up not only Indonesia but Guam, Midway and the Philippines. The success of the widespread operation depended on greatly disabling and thoroughly discouraging America's Pacific Fleet. That charge fell to Nagumo and his immense oceangoing force of six aircraft carriers, two battleships, three cruisers and nine destroyers.

That Nagumo's armada made its way undetected from Hitokappu Bay to within striking distance of Pearl Harbor borders on the miraculous. Maintaining strict radio silence for more than a week, the ships sailed north at approximately 43 degrees latitude, seeking less-traveled waters. They hit stormy seas. They plowed through fog. They made their way.

Three large submarines surged ahead as scouts. Twenty-seven other subs also traversed the ocean, their aim to surround Oahu and attack anything that attempted to escape the harbor. Five of these vessels bore midget submarines that would zip into Pearl Harbor before the attack began.

The strike force settled 230 miles north of Oahu, and from there, on December 7, 1941, at 6 a.m.,

the first wave of 183 planes—49 Kate bombers, each armed with one 1,760-pound armor-piercing bomb; 40 Kates carrying torpedoes; 51 Val dive bombers, each of which carried a 551-pound bomb; and 43 Zero fighter planes—were launched from the carriers and roared toward Hawaii.

At 7:49 a.m., Air Group Commander Fuchida Mitsuo spotted Pearl Harbor: seven battleships in Battleship Row. At 7:53, he gave the signal by telegraph key: *to* and *ra*—or together, the word for "tiger." Over and over: *to-ra, to-ra, to-ra.*

The torpedo bombers dived to a level from which they would launch their weapons. Other bombers split off to hit Army and Navy airfields. The biggest planes flew steadily on, homing in on their targets. The Zeros, having swept down Oahu's west coast, prepared to strafe and bedevil. Their job as escorts was done, and they instantly shifted into gear as fighter planes.

Below, sailors were preparing for the 8 a.m. hoisting of the colors aboard the great ships. They saw the torpedo bombers screaming earthward. They saw the lethal shells in the water, incoming. A bomb exploded in the bay. The torpedoes sped toward the ships.

At 7:58, the alarm went out: "Air raid, Pearl Harbor. This is not drill!" Within minutes the *West Virginia, Nevada, Oklahoma* and *California* had been struck by torpedoes. War was on.

Top left: Zeros waited on the carrier *Akagi,* their engines revving, prior to departing for Pearl Harbor. A brilliantly engineered plane—superior to any U.S. fighter at the time—the Zero (known as a "Zeke") could also function as a bomber. Zeros were the planes that first launched the attack. Owing to heavy seas, takeoffs were difficult from ships that were listing as much as 15 degrees, but there could be no delays that might snarl the complex strategy. Above: A "Kate," Japan's principal torpedo bomber, lifted off from the *Shokaku,* bound for Pearl.

Autumn, 1941: All is quiet on the western front. This aerial view of Pearl Harbor faces southwest, with the Pacific Ocean in the distance. (Note that the orientation differs from the maps on the following pages, which are set due north.) The Ford Island Naval Air Station is in the center of the harbor, and the Navy Yard is just above and to the left. Moored on the upper-left side of Ford Island, behind two battleships, is the aircraft carrier *Enterprise,* one of the most celebrated American vessels of the Second World War. If that ship, or other carriers, had been caught at Pearl on December 7, a very different saga might have unfolded in the Pacific theater.

U.S. Navy

These three maps provide a telescoped portrait of the attack on Pearl Harbor. The overview at **left** shows the route of the 31 Japanese ships, which included six aircraft carriers, before and after the bombing. The small orange arrow indicates the 230-mile journey that the planes took to reach Oahu. That island is represented in the map **below**; the arrows indicate the primary flight paths of incoming Japanese aircraft. (Bombing, of course, was not strictly confined to those paths.) The square at the bottom of the Oahu map is magnified at **right**: Pearl Harbor as it existed at the moment of the attack.

N

U.S.S.R.

Manchuria

JAPAN

Kobe

Tokyo

Refueling Point Dec. 3

Hitokappu Bay Rendezvous Nov. 22 Sortie Nov. 26

Route of the Pearl Harbor Strike Force

Midway Islands

Launching Point Dec. 7

Marcus Island

Wake Island

Planes recovered

Oahu Hawaii

Dec. 16 Part of the Strike Force breaks off to support attack on Wake Island

Philippine Islands

Guam

PACIFIC OCEAN

PACIFIC OCEAN

First Attack 183 Aircraft 7:55 a.m.

Second Attack 168 Aircraft 8:54 a.m.

51 Dive-bombers

Opana Mobile Radar Station

Haleiwa Field

36 Fighters

54 High-level Bombers

78 Dive-bombers

25

O A H U

Schofield Barracks

Wheeler Field

40 Torpedo Bombers

43 Fighters

14

11

26

19

17

9

Kaneohe

18

Pearl Harbor
AREA OF MAP ON RIGHT

16

49 High-level Bombers

24

Ewa Field

Hickam Field

Fort Shafter

18

Bellows Field

Honolulu

27

3 MILES

Ramsay
Gamble
Montgomery
Trever

Breese
Zane
Perry
Wasm

WAIPIO PENINSULA

Model © Robert D. Bracci

Monaghan
Farragut
Dale
Aylwin

Henley
Patterson
Ralph Talbot

Selfridge
Case
Tucker
Reid
Conyngham
Whitney

Blue

Phoenix

PEARL
CITY

Phelps
MacDonough
Worden
Dewey
Hull
Dobbin

Pearl Harbor
December 7, 1941

KEY TO SHIPS
Sunk
Heavy damage
Moderate damage
No damage

Solace

Tangier

Utah Raleigh Detroit

Allen
Chew

usa

Curtiss

F O R D
I S L A N D

Maryland Tennessee Arizona Nevada
Oklahoma W.Virginia Vestal

B A T T L E S H I P   R O W

Pearl Harbor
Naval Air
Station

Neosho

California

Seaplane
Base

Avocet

Argonne
Sacramento

Ramapo
New Orleans
San Francisco
St. Louis
Honolulu

Pelias

Shaw

Downes
Cassin
Pennsylvania

Cachalot

Oglala
Helena

Bagley

Submarine
Base

Sumner

Castor

Oil Storage
Tanks

Hospital
Point

Navy Yard

Coaling
Station

Oil Storage
Tanks

Helm

Hickam
Field

海軍省許可濟第二八十號

This photo of Ford Island, facing roughly east, was taken from a Japanese plane minutes after the attack had begun. On the far side of the island, in Battleship Row, water and smoke gushed from the *West Virginia,* which had just been torpedoed, and from the *Oklahoma* (listing to port). On the near side (second and third from left), the light cruiser *Raleigh* and target ship *Utah* (mistaken for a battleship) had caught torpedoes. Two Kate torpedo bombers are visible, one over Battleship Row and the other over the Navy Yard, at right rear. This picture was seized after the war—note the Japanese writing at the bottom. Above: Surrounded but unharmed by antiaircraft fire, a "Val" dive-bomber banked.

03:42 Ensign R.C. McCloy, aboard the minesweeper **Condor**, spots a periscope in the darkness.

03:57 The **Condor** sends a message to the destroyer **Ward**: "Sighted submerged submarine on westerly course, speed 9 knots."

06:00 The first wave of the Japanese attack takes off for Hawaii from ships anchored north of the islands.

06:26 Japanese pilots bound for Pearl see the sun rise, and the vivid shafts of light bring to mind their naval flag.

06:45 After searching for hours, the **Ward** fires depth charges and sinks the Japanese sub.

It was about 8 a.m. in this Japanese photo, and the attack on Battleship Row was getting under way. (Note plane in circle.) Torpedoes can be seen streaking for the ships, which were, from left: the *Nevada*, *Arizona* (repair ship *Vestal* lay on outside), *West Virginia* outside of *Tennessee,* and *Oklahoma* outside of *Maryland*. The *California* (at far right), *Oklahoma* and *West Virginia* have been hit, as evidenced by ripples and spreading oil. The *West Virginia* was saved from capsizing when quick thinking by Lt. Claude V. Ricketts led to counterflooding measures that let the ship settle to the bottom on an even keel. The white smoke at rear issued from Hickam Field, the gray smoke from the light cruiser *Helena*.

07:02 Privates Joseph Lockard and George Elliott pick up blips on radar. They are told by a superior that what they have spotted is an incoming flight of American planes.

07:49 Commander Fuchida Mitsuo, the head of the assault, issues the attack signal as his plane passes just off Lahilahi Point. Four minutes later he calls out, "Tora! Tora! Tora!"—code words confirming that the Japanese have surprised their enemy.

07:55 The raid begins at Pearl Harbor as the **Raleigh, Helena, Utah** and **Oklahoma** are struck. Years later, in an interview with Ronald E. Marcello of the University of North Texas Oral History Program, Seaman Garlen W. Eslick of the **Oklahoma** recalls, "This boy just slumped over. Blood was all over everything. I still didn't know what had happened ... I heard this thing roar over ...

the officer-of-the-deck came on and announced, 'Man your battle stations.'"

07:56 There are two explosions on the **Arizona**. Pfc. James Cory: "The bridge shielded us from flames ... Around the edges in these open windows came the heat and the sensation of the blast. We cringed there ... I think that at this moment I wanted to flee, but this was impossible. You're on station, you're in combat."

07:58 As bombs explode on Ford Island, Lt. Comdr. Logan Ramsey hurries to the radio room and sends the message, "Air raid, Pearl Harbor. This is not drill!" Yeoman 1c. Leonard Webb rushes to get his wife and child to a car: "When we're almost to the car, my wife says, 'The baby doesn't have any diapers! Get some!' Here's the humor. Bear in mind that this is Armageddon, the end of the world, and my wife has me chasing diapers!"

A Japanese horizontal bomber captured this early view of Battleship Row (left, from bottom): the *Nevada,* torpedoed and enveloped in smoke; *Vestal,* outside of *Arizona,* which had just been hit; *West Virginia* and *Oklahoma* (outside of *Tennessee* and *Maryland*), listing and oozing oil. Above: Minutes later, the *Arizona* exploded.

At 8:06 a.m., the forward magazines of the *Arizona* were struck by a bomb, setting off shock waves that were felt by planes 10,000 feet above. In that instant, some 1,000 men perished, three of whom would receive the Medal of Honor. **Right:** The *Arizona,* engulfed in furious flames and smoke in late morning, would burn for two days. The explosion caused the front upper portion of the ship to collapse into the hull; thus the forward superstructure tilted 45 degrees and forward guns hovered just above the waterline. **At near left:** Sailors on the stern of the *Tennessee* manned water hoses to keep burning oil away from their ship. **Above:** a frame from a film shot aboard the hospital ship *Solace,* which treated many of the *Arizona*'s casualties.

08:01 Ensign Joseph K. Taussig Jr. sounds the **Nevada**'s general quarters and rushes to his battle station. Injured as his ship is strafed, Taussig continues his work.

08:02 Twenty-five bombers dive toward Wheeler Field. "The sailor approximately six feet in front of me fell," says Pvt. Leslie Le Fan. "I stepped over him, and remember thinking to myself: 'That's the first dead man I have ever seen.'"

08:03 Machine and antiaircraft guns aboard the **Cummings**, **California**, **Swan** and the submarine **Cachalot** open fire.

The attack was only minutes old, and the *Utah* (left) already strained at her mooring ropes en route to capsizing. The *Utah* had been converted to a training and target ship, which was well known to Japanese airmen, whose instructions to ignore the vessel vanished in the heat of the moment. Right: In this Japanese photo, the *Utah* (second from bottom) had gone belly-up. Other ships included, from top, the light cruisers *Detroit,* which was strafed but not damaged, and *Raleigh,* listing to port after a torpedo hit. The seaplane tender *Tangier* (bottom) suffered superficial damage from a near-miss bomb.

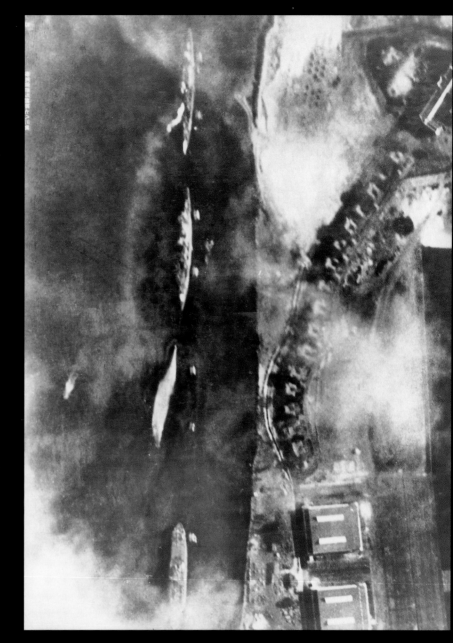

08:06 A 1,763-lb. missile fired by PO Kanai Noboru hits the **Arizona**. It demolishes the forward magazine and kills nearly 1,000 men. "It was so vivid in my mind," says Private Le Fan, who saw the action from the Marine barracks. "[The **Arizona**] just quivered, buckled and then settled. It looked like ... well, that killed it ... It was so devastating."

08:08 Two bombs strike the **West Virginia**, whose captain, Mervyn Bennion, is mortally wounded by a piece of shrapnel that flies over from the **Tennessee**. "A huge waterspout splashed over the stack of the ship and then tumbled down like an exhausted geyser," recalls Japanese commander Matsumura Midori, who fired one of the torpedoes that hit the

ship. "What a magnificent sight." Webley Edwards at KGMB radio announces: "All Army, Navy and Marine personnel to report to duty." As Water Tender 2c. Emil T. Beran closes the hatch behind him on board the **Allen**, he says, "God save us! This is the last time that I'm ever going to see the sunshine!" Beran will ultimately survive the attack.

08:10 (13:40 E.S.T.) In Washington, President Roosevelt is informed by Navy Secretary Frank Knox that there has been a sneak attack on Pearl Harbor. This is "just the kind of unexpected thing the Japanese would do," says FDR. "[A]t the very time they were discussing peace in the Pacific, they were plotting to overthrow it."

Wheeler Field, the Army air base in central Oahu, was under heavy attack in this Japanese photo taken during the first wave. Dive-bombers and Zeros laid waste to hangars, barracks and more than half of the 153 planes there. General Walter Short's preoccupation with sabotage led to planes being stored outside in plain sight—in neat rows perfect for the attackers. Only a handful of the 82 fighters got off the ground. In any case, many of them were obsolete and all of them had their ammo belts removed every night. Right: In one of the few action pictures of personnel fighting back, three Marines at Ewa Field looked for a place from which to fire, while two others looked for something to fire at

08:12 The **Utah** capsizes. "By the time I got to the door, the ship rolled over," says Seaman 2c. John Vaessen. "Well, I'm hanging on to everything—the door and anything I could grab—and the deck plates come flying at me, fire extinguishers—everything loose—and I was hit in many places but no sharp edges … I was just lucky that God was with me, that's for sure."

08:14 Americans set up machine guns at Wheeler Field and fire at Japanese planes, bringing down one Zero. "I helped to give the sacraments to the dying and aid to the suffering," says Father Marcus Valenta. "They had boys lying out on the lawn in front of a little first-aid station."

08:15 Rescue workers pull men out of the burning water. "Our own oil was bubbling up and congealing," says Pfc. James Cory of the **Arizona**. "People who have never seen this at sea cannot imagine what oil is like once it is exposed to cool seawater … It was catching fire slowly and was incinerating toward us."

08:17 The destroyer **Helm** clears the harbor, spots a Japanese submarine and fires on it—missing.

08:25 At Schofield Barracks, Lt. Stephen Saltzman and Sgt. Lowell Klatt grab rifles and fire at a Zero as it strafes them. The men keep shooting until the plane crashes.

08:25 Japanese planes attack Hawaiian firemen at Hickam Field, killing three. "They were so low you could see them grinning," says Machinist Mate 2c. Leon Bennett. "They were laughing, all smiles."

The Japanese Val dive-bombers at right were photographed from one of a dozen B-17s bound for the Philippines, with a scheduled first stop at Hickam Field. They arrived in the middle of the fracas, but had set out without ammo to save fuel for the long trip from California. All the planes landed safely except Capt. Raymond Swenson's (above), which broke in two as it crash-landed after a Japanese shell set off magnesium flares in the radio compartment. This was the expected group of B-17s that had led to the squelching of earlier radar reports of incoming aircraft.

08:30 Sailors on the **Downes** open fire on attacking planes. "We had the .50-caliber machine guns," recalls Gunner's Mate 2c. Curtis Schulze. "They were water-cooled, and some of the men worried about the water, and I said, 'To hell with the damned water! Don't worry about it! Just start firing the goddamned things!'"

08:35 A number of U.S. planes returning from a scouting mission see that they cannot land on Ford Island. They head instead for Ewa Field to the west, where the Japanese have damaged or destroyed all 47 Marine planes. When one of the planes touches the ground, a Marine runs out and shouts, "For God's sake, get into the air or they'll strafe you too!" The plane manages to take off again.

08:35 The first wave of the attack ends. "Amputees. They started coming in, and they had arms and legs just shot off—a terrible mass of tissues, bones, blood," recalls 2d Lt. Elizabeth Murphy, a nurse at Tripler General Hospital. "Oh, heavens! I had never seen anything like this!"

Pearl Harbor, 9 a.m. The second attack was at full throttle, but by now American defenses had awakened and were sending up this mass of antiaircraft fire. A huge, billowing column of smoke spewed from the stricken *Arizona*. The smoke left of the *Arizona* came from the destroyers *Shaw*, *Cassin* and *Downes*, which were in dry dock at the Navy Yard. The photo was taken from the hills northwest of the harbor.

At approximately the time of the second wave, sailors in all manner of dress at the Naval Air Station on Ford Island reloaded ammunition clips and belts—and kept an eye out for the new enemy. Above: A Val dive-bomber, hit by antiaircraft fire during that second wave, was moments away from crashing into the seaplane tender *Curtiss*.

08:47 The destroyer **Blue** gets under way, with Ens. Nathan F. Asher at the helm. When two planes dive toward the ship, sailors respond with .50-caliber machine guns. (Asher later says he had no idea how the men "got their ammunition from the magazines to the guns in the fast and swift manner that they did.") After they down a Japanese plane, crewmen on the **Blue** stop shooting and pat one another on the back.

08:50 The battleship **Nevada** heads out, in part because the wounded Ensign Taussig has managed to start the second boiler. The Japanese spot the ship leaving the harbor and determine to sink her, hoping to block the channel. "The Japanese bombers swarmed down on us like bees," recalls Lt. Lawrence Ruff.

08:50 (14:20 E.S.T.) In Washington, Secretary of State Cordell Hull, well aware of what is transpiring in Hawaii, erupts when given a note from the Japanese breaking off peace talks: "I have never seen a document that was more crowded with infamous falsehoods and distortions—on a scale so huge that I never imagined until today that any government on this planet was capable of uttering them."

This was the view from Pier One of the Submarine Base, looking toward the Navy Yard, at about 9:15 a.m. Sailors in the foreground, with rifles and pistol belts, crouched as they searched for enemy aircraft. To their left was the sub *Narwhal* and at far left, the *Dolphin*. Coming from the right was the oiler *Neosho,* which had escaped from Battleship Row with her perilous cargo of aviation fuel.

08:54 The second wave of the Japanese attack, this one under the command of Lt. Comdr. Shimazaki Shigekazu, swarms over Pearl. Fifty-four high-level bombers and 78 dive-bombers spread out to hit ships, airfields and barracks throughout Oahu, while 36 fighters maintain air control.

09:00 A formation of Zeros strikes Bellows Field, blowing up a gasoline truck and hitting a plane from the 44th squadron as it tries to take off. Just in case anyone on the island remains unconvinced, KGMB radio's Edwards blurts over the air, "This is the real McCoy!"

09:05 At Wheeler Field, 27 Japanese planes attack aircraft that are parked on the ground. The Japanese also strike barracks, service buildings and a baseball field.

09:06 A bomb hits the **Downes** while she sits in dry dock. Another strikes Adm. Husband E. Kimmel's flagship, the **Pennsylvania**, detonating guns and ammunition.

09:07 An order is issued instructing Americans to cease firing on U.S. B-17s that are attempting to land at Hickam Field.

Of the many instances of bravery at Pearl, one of the most visible was the *Nevada*'s attempt to sortie, or depart from the harbor. Blasted during the first wave, and threatened by fiery oil spilling from the *Arizona,* the *Nevada* made for the open seas at about 9 a.m. (above). The sight of the gallant ship electrified and emboldened Americans on the shore. Minutes later, under withering fire, the ship beached itself (below) rather than bottle up the harbor. Right: Sailors manned the guns on the seaplane tender *Avocet* in the foreground, while the *Nevada* (center), her bow in flames, had been swung around by harbor currents.

The forward magazines of the destroyer *Shaw* took a direct hit as she lay in floating dry dock. The impact of three 550-lb. bombs tore off the entire bow of the ship. The explosives might have been meant for the *Nevada* (gun turrets visible at lower right), already beached for 20 minutes. The picture above was taken only seconds later from an air base on Ford Island, where sailors, standing amid a squadron of wrecked planes, watched the fireball from the *Shaw* ascend.

09:08 Dive-bombers attack the **Raleigh**; one bomb misses the ship's aviation tanks by mere feet. "A lot of times planes were coming at us from all angles," remembers Seaman 1c. Nick L. Kouretas, a gunner. "I'd try to concentrate on one target. They'd say: 'Get this guy!' you know, and I'd lead him, hoping I could get him. I know I was scared as hell."

09:10 In order not to block the channel that leads out of the harbor, Lt. Comdr. J.F. Thomas beaches the wounded **Nevada** at Hospital Point.

09:15 Captain J.W. Bunkley, who has spent the night ashore, returns to the **California**. The ship has been hit numerous times and is in flames. "If we had had a 15-minute warning, we could have been partially prepared to defend ourselves," says Seaman Jerod Haynes. "Anything would have beaten [being] a sittin' duck." Within an hour, Bunkley is forced to abandon his ship.

09:20 A bomb passes through the dock alongside the cruiser **Honolulu**. It explodes underwater, flooding part of the ship and damaging her oil tanks.

Not every ship at Pearl Harbor was damaged in the attack. In this picture, taken at 9:26 from a moving car north of the harbor, there are two groups of destroyers and their tenders, all of which survived without harm.

09:28 Gunners aboard the **Mugford** shoot down a Japanese bomber after it pulls out of its dive alongside the ship's port bow.

09:30 In the ships' logs of the **Antares** and **Whitney,** it is noted that the attack may be over. Years later, Seaman Eslick tells the Oral History Program what it was like to be trapped aboard the **Oklahoma:** "You did a little praying and thinking things. You think about your family. I had a younger sister who was just a baby. I thought about my brothers and all my family. Would I ever see them again? But I never once ... thought that I was going to die ... I knew I was in one heck of a predicament ... I was hoping I would get out. I knew what kind of situation I was in, and I came to the conclusion of what I was up against ... With all these fumes and stuff, my eyes were burning. I had saltwater, gasoline, bunker oil and stuff all in my eyes; and I'd swallowed I don't know how much saltwater ... We stayed in that compartment rapping out this SOS. I don't know how long it was. We could hear the boys, some of them, in this one compartment next to us, and they were hollering for help for a good long time. There wasn't anything we could do about it, and then they became quiet. They evidently drowned."

U.S. Navy

National Archives

At Kaneohe Naval Air Station, a sailor sprinted past burning PBY patrol planes. Kaneohe was strafed in the first wave, then hit with high-level bombing. Later strafing finished the job. The toll was fearsome: Of the 36 planes stationed there, 30 were destroyed. The only three that survived intact were in the air at the time of the assault. Above: The Seaplane Base on the southwest point of Ford Island was one of the earliest targets. This picture of Seaplane Hangar No. 6 may have been taken during the second wave. At lower left, men with rifles scanned the skies.

09:37 A large explosion on the battleship **Cassin** causes her to roll over onto the **Downes**.

09:40 The flames on the **West Virginia** reach as high as the foretop. Wounded are being removed from the ship.

09:41 "It was noted by everyone participating in action that after an hour or more heavy thirst was experienced requiring considerable drinking water," notes the ship's log of the **Pennsylvania**. "This confirms the necessity of having water at all battle stations."

09:43 Sailors aboard the **Tern** pull survivors out of the water. They will rescue 47 in all.

09:50 The **Blue** picks up the signal of a submarine. She maneuvers to attack and then drops six depth charges. An oil slick and air bubbles rise to the surface. The ship then detects another signal from a submarine that appears to be bearing down on the **St. Louis**. That sub, too, is sunk by a depth charge.

10:00 The Japanese first wave returns, victorious and exultant, to its aircraft carriers north of Hawaii.

U.S. Navy

From on high, a bomber savored the view during the second wave. In the foreground is Hickam Field, which has been pounded. The black smoke at right center rose from Battleship Row, where the capsized *Oklahoma* is visible. The listing *California* is at left, and the black smoke to her left issued from the *Shaw*. Below Battleship Row, the oiler *Neosho* steamed toward the Submarine Base.

10:00 Robert Shivers, head of the FBI's Honolulu bureau, places a guard at the Japanese consulate. Elsewhere, wounded are being attended to, dead are being found. Seaman 1c. Nick L. Kouretas of the **Raleigh** is looking frantically for his brother: "Every time we brought a load over to the landing, I would jump off and run up the landing, because they were laying them like cordwood, a body here and a body there, with a walkway down the center where they would try to identify them by their dog tags, with their heads pointing into the walkway. I would run along the aisle and, knowing my brother's characteristics, look for him. He chewed his nails. I knew where he had a wart; I knew every little mark on his body. I would get so far, and I'd say, 'Well, this guy looks like him,' but I couldn't see his face. I'd pick up a hand, and I'd say, 'No, that's not him,' and then go on." Seaman Kouretas's brother survived the attack.

10:04 A Japanese midget sub shoots two torpedoes at the **St. Louis**, which has made its way clear of the channel. Captain George Rood reacts and has the ship change course; the torpedoes strike near the harbor's entrance. Sailors fire at the sub when it surfaces.

Koku—Fan Magazine

THE ATTACK **LIFE**

Two battleships under siege: The *West Virginia* (center, foreground), shredded by bombs and torpedoes, was on fire and sinking. Behind her, the *Tennessee* was struck by two bombs but would emerge from repairs in May 1943 and go on to participate in some of the most critical actions in the war, from Tarawa to Okinawa. At far left, the hull of the *Oklahoma* is visible behind rescue boats.

10:05 Hawaii's Governor Joseph Poindexter calls local newspapers to announce a state of emergency for the entire territory.

10:10 As an uneasy sense that the air attack has ended spreads throughout Oahu, ships report and mobilize—even as sailors keep watch for a third wave of planes. The **Reid** reports that it has suffered no damage or casualties, and gets under way.

10:20 Rumors are everywhere. A U.S. attack group of 15 VSBs, each carrying half-ton bombs, is sent to scout 30 miles south of Pearl, as there have been reports of enemy carriers and possible landing forces.

10:23 The **Wasmuth** drops one depth charge. There are no signs that it hits any subs.

10:30 To the west, at Japanese Imperial headquarters in Tokyo, it is announced that Japan is now at war with the United States of America.

10:36 The **Wasmuth** drops another depth charge, and this time a spread of oil and bubbles indicates a hit.

11:27 Four A-20s join the search for enemy vessels reported to the south.

Nimitz Museum

control flooding wrought by the torpedo warheads.

11:35 The **Breese** picks up the sound of a submarine and drops two depth charges. Soon after, an oil slick appears, followed by debris. The **Breese** continues the attack by dropping four more depth charges. Destroyers in the area hurry to the scene to make certain that the sub has been destroyed. Even as most of the Japanese air strike force is safe on carriers many miles to the north, ready to head for home, Japanese submariners remain vulnerable in Pearl Harbor.

11:42 Believing that the Japanese have used—and perhaps are still using—radio signals to home in on the area, the U.S. Army orders all local stations off the air. Only special announcements may be aired.

11:46 Japanese troops are again reported to be landing on Oahu—another of many false sightings.

12:10 Pilots led by Lt. Comdr. Halstead Hopping set out for an area 200 miles north of Hawaii, searching for the Japanese.

12:21 It is reported that there are nine unidentified aircraft over Guam. The Japanese do, in fact, attack that island on December 7.

12:30 Honolulu police raid the Japanese embassy. They find consulate members burning coded books in a washtub. The police also seize a large envelope filled with undestroyed papers. At this point, all is still confusion, and there is no telling what might be invaluable or incriminating.

13:00 Commander Fuchida lands aboard the **Akagi**. His is the last plane to return to the Japanese carriers.

U.S. Navy

In the bowels of hell: The *California* was concealed in the ferocious black smoke at left. The battleship visible at center is the *Maryland.* In the cruel tapestry of smoke behind her, the lighter color likely issued from the *Arizona,* and the darker plume at center was mainly from the *West Virginia.* To the right of that can be seen the white hull of the capsized *Oklahoma.* On the far right, beyond the cement mooring quay, a harbor tug directed a spout of water toward the inferno. To the left of the tug, small rescue craft braved the burning oil in search of survivors.

13:12 The U.S. Army reports that four enemy transports are off Barbers Point to the southwest of Pearl Harbor, thus continuing the day's stream of erroneous intelligence.

13:30 Hawaii's territorial director of civil defense orders nighttime blackouts. Meanwhile, many miles to the north, signal flags are waved aboard the Japanese aircraft carrier **Akagi**, setting in motion the fleet's withdrawal from the region.

15:00 Officers aboard the **Tennessee** pick up a report that Wake Island has been attacked by as many as 30 Japanese bombers.

16:25 Governor Poindexter institutes martial law on all Hawaiian islands.

16:28 As search and rescue efforts continue throughout the harbor, the fire on the **West Virginia** is reported to be finally under control.

21:00 U.S. bombers arriving at Oahu from the aircraft carrier **Enterprise**—which has been on maneuvers away from Pearl Harbor, and which will subsequently play a crucial and heroic role in the Pacific war—are mistaken by American ground troops for enemy planes, and are fired upon. "You could have read a newspaper by the tracer bullets," remembers Seaman Virgle Wilkerson.

21:14 A report from the stores-and-supply ship **Antares** says that the glare in Pearl Harbor is getting brighter as fires grow in intensity.

This view looks down Pier 1010 toward the Navy Yard's dry docks. In the foreground, the ancient minelayer *Oglala* lay on her side after being smashed by adjacent explosions on the cruiser *Helena,* here moored to *Oglala*'s left. The *Oglala* had occupied the usual berth of the battleship *Pennsylvania,* whose mast is visible beyond the *Helena* and in front of smoke from the burning destroyers *Cassin* and *Downes.* The billowing smoke at right came from the *Shaw,* whose stern is visible in the floating dry dock. On the far right is the *Nevada,* beached and aflame.

05:15 (December 8, morning) Hawaiian police erroneously report enemy parachute troops landing in Kaliki Valley. "We each had our rifles loaded," says Private Le Fan, who the day before had seen a man cut down right in front of him at Wheeler Field. "We had our pistols loaded, and we were given orders to shoot anything that moved."

05:17 Submarines are sighted off Diamond Head. "A thing that kept going through my mind was: 'Oh, hell! They are going to land!'" says Machinist Mate 2c. Leon Bennett of the **Neosho.** "There was no way we could have kept a landing force from invading ... [N]ot only the Navy but the Army and Marines were all totally disorganized."

06:45 Police radio reports that all schools are closed, and urges citizens to stay home. Years later, Dan Wentrcek, who was a fireman third class on the **Nevada,** recalls the atmosphere of December 8 in an interview with the University of North Texas Pearl Harbor Oral History Program: "We went back out the next day and tried to clean up ... They took a group of us for burial detail on Aiea Landing. We worked over there as they would pick up bodies ... They'd find them floating out in the water, and they'd bring them over, or the pieces, and then they had pharmacist's mates over there who would take fingerprints if they were unidentifiable ... [T]hey brought the bodies in, and we had a bunch of pine boxes there that'd been made up ... If they needed some help, why, we'd help them put a body in a box, and they would give it a number. A lot of times they had a bunch of pieces. We'd just have to put them in a box."

National Archives

At the south end of the Seaplane Base PBY ramp on Ford Island, Marines and sailors scoured the afternoon sky for signs of the enemy. They were surrounded by sandbags and parts of wrecked PBYs. In the background, the *Nevada* is beached at Waipio Point; tugs had taken her there after she ran aground at Hospital Point.

These two aerial photos provide an overview of the damage done. Left: Battleship Row lay in ruin. At bottom is the *Arizona,* and ahead of her the sunken *West Virginia* was outside the lightly damaged *Tennessee.* To free the "Big Tenn," the Navy Yard had to dynamite her forward quay. Ahead of the *Tennessee* was the *Maryland,* and outside of her rested the capsized *Oklahoma,* with a barge alongside to assist ongoing rescue efforts. In the upper-left corner, the *California,* sunk, was surrounded by smaller vessels. Below: This view of the Navy Yard shows dry dock activity. At the top, the *Shaw,* her bow blown off, lay at an angle in the floating dry dock. Beneath her the torpedoed *Helena* was in for repairs. Below the *Helena* was the *Pennsylvania,* and to her left the wrecked destroyers *Downes* and *Cassin.* In both of these photographs, dark oil streaks infiltrate the harbor.

These two pages correlate with the aerial view on pages 110–111; thus, Battleship Row is on the left, and dry dock is on the right. There, the *Cassin* has been slammed over onto the *Downes*. Both destroyers were eventually rebuilt but required new hulls. Behind them was the *Pennsylvania*, which sustained relatively light damage despite being a sitting duck. The crane at right was operated by civilian yard worker George Walters, who had moved the device back and forth during the attack in an effort to divert low-flying planes from the battleship. Above: A barge helped with rescue work at the *Oklahoma*. Left: The carcass of the *Arizona*.

皇紀二千六百三年
水垣正義筆

Yamamoto had a secret weapon for Pearl Harbor: five midget submarines strapped behind the conning towers of normal subs and towed within range. Each was 78-ft. long by 6-ft. wide and carried two torpedoes and two crewmen. There never seemed to be any hope, though, that they would be able to inflict real damage; this was basically a suicide mission. Nine of the men in these subs died and were commemorated in the silk painting above, with Ford Island in the center. They became national heroes in Japan, owing to reports that a midget sub had sunk the *Arizona*. The 10th submariner, Sakamaki Kazuo, commanded the sub at left. Because he survived (opposite), he officially ceased to exist.

Sakamaki's sub (opposite) suffered from a failed gyroscope and was uncontrollable. Eventually he (and a crewman who died) abandoned ship and washed ashore near Bellows Field, where Sgt. David M. Akui made him America's first prisoner of war in World War II. Note the alterations in the form at right, and that one mug shot is a modified version of the photo below.

BASIC PERSONNEL RECORD

INTERNED ALIEN ENEMY

PRISONER OF WAR

Recast ... on improper form. New read complete

| SAKAMAKI | Kazuo | | ISN-HJ-1-MI | Kazuo Sakamaki |
| Surname | Given Name | Middle Name | Serial Number | Signature |

Hostile Unit Army — Submarine Service (Two man) Japanese Co.G - 298th INF.
Nationality Arresting Agency

Hostile Rank: Sub Lieutenant   Hostile Service: Naval   Capturing Unit

Hostile Serial No. Refused to answer. 0540 8th December 1941, Bellows Field, Hawaii
Home Address Time and place of first Capture

Person to be notified in emergency:
Refused to disclose. Notify Navy Department, Tokyo, Japan.
Name Address Relationship

Dependents:
Name Sex Age Address
None

Home Address: Tokushima Ken, Town of Hayashi, Japan.

Japanese; some Chinese   Naval Officer   Graduate of Japanese Naval Academy.
Languages Spoken   Profession   Education

PHYSICAL DESCRIPTION

Age 24 Date of Birth 17 Nov. Sex Male
1917
Place of Birth Tokushima,Ken; town of
Hayashi,Japan. Comp. Yellow Hair Black
Height 63¾"
Weight 131 Eyes Brown Build Stocky

Scars and Marks Three burn scars under each eye.

KAZUO SAKAMAKI ISN HJ 1 MI

KAZUO SAKAMAKI ISN HJ 1 MI

The U.S. forces suffered staggering losses, but when they fought back, it was with a vengeance. Perhaps the spirit of the day—and of the long years to come—was best exemplified by Navy Chaplain Howell Forgy on the cruiser *New Orleans* when he exhorted the men, "Praise the Lord and pass the ammunition!" Twenty-nine Japanese planes were shot from the skies, including this dive-bomber (above) from the carrier *Kaga*, which had been piloted by Lt. Suzuki Mimori. Left: These aviator's rations were found in a downed plane. Right: This Japanese pilot washed up on shore.

As it is true that every soldier knows that he or she may have to make the ultimate sacrifice, so it is true that in every war, civilians, too, will perish. In Honolulu on December 7, these stretcher-bearers rushed a casualty to a makeshift aid station on the grounds of the Lunalilo School, on Pumehana Street. The roof of the school had been set on fire, perhaps by shells from antiaircraft guns. In all, 68 civilians were killed in the attack; another 35 were wounded.

The island of Oahu was filled with death and destruction on that fateful day. Honolulu, just a few miles from Pearl Harbor, was clobbered by antiaircraft shells from American guns that had missed their mark. Ordinarily, time fuses on the shells made them burst in the air; in the chaos of the attack, many fuses weren't set, and the shells detonated when they hit the ground. There were explosions all over the city. Above: At the intersection of McCully and King streets, volunteer firemen fed a hose to a man on this rooftop. Below: The Japanese plane that crashed into this house—where a Japanese family resided—was one of the first to be shot down. Right: An antiaircraft shell landed near this Packard in Honolulu, killing three men from Kaneohe who were headed for their jobs at Pearl Harbor.

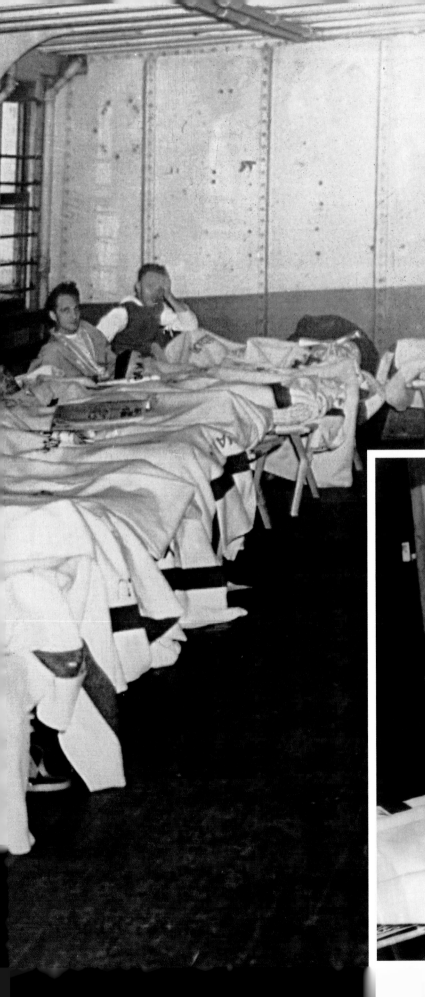

These pictures appeared in *The New York Times* on January 1, 1942. The headline read: TRANSPORTS BRING MORE FROM HAWAII. The story, by Lawrence E. Davies, was datelined San Francisco. It began: "In the last hours of 1941, as the Pacific Coast stayed 'on the alert' against possible holiday surprises by the enemy from sea and air, scores of men wounded in the Japanese raid on Pearl Harbor were brought through the Golden Gate, the second batch of Army and Navy casualties to reach the mainland ... Smiling or grim, as they hobbled with crutches or were carried on stretchers from transports, the soldiers and sailors, even those with serious injuries from bomb fragments or bullets, appealed to doctors to 'fix us up quick,' for 'there's work to be done out there next year.' ... Some of the wounded recounted their experiences ... Typical was the story of J. R. Trammell, aged 20, a farm boy from Oklahoma, who raised his arm on the stretcher as he spoke ... 'I was in the crew's galley, and that's where I got mine—shrapnel in both legs. All five boys with me were hit ... I'm ready to go back right now.'"

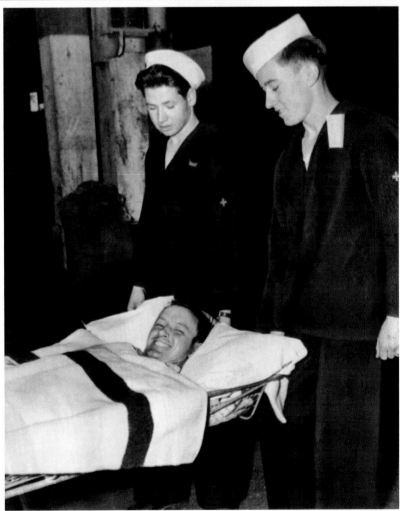

In the days after the attack, grim discoveries were made everywhere in and around Pearl Harbor, while clues to what had happened were sought behind closed doors. Sailors trapped in the hulls of ships, some of them ill from having lain in pools of oil and water, were rescued. Bodies washed ashore, including this American sailor on the shore of Kaneohe Bay. Meanwhile, on December 11, Secretary of State Knox arrived on the scene. He met with military officers, then departed the next day to report to FDR. His harsh assessment of the preparedness at Pearl, and his descriptions of "the shambles of the Battle Line of the world's mightiest fleet," led to the replacement of both Admiral Kimmel and General Short.

WESTERN UNION

CLASS OF SERVICE

This is a full-rate Telegram or Cablegram unless its deferred character is indicated by a suitable symbol above or preceding the address.

R. B. WHITE
PRESIDENT

NEWCOMB CARLTON
CHAIRMAN OF THE BOARD

J. C. WILLEVER
FIRST VICE-PRESIDENT

1220

SYMBOLS

DL=Day Letter

NL=Night Letter

LC=Deferred Cable

NLT=Cable Night Letter

Ship Radiogram

The filing time shown in the date line on telegrams and day letters is STANDARD TIME at point of origin.   Time of receipt is STANDARD TIME at point of destination

LDT1MM 80 GOVT

WASHINGTON DC 1204A DEC 21 1941

MRS GENEVIEVE DUNLAP

3545 LINDA VISTA TERRACE LOSA

THE NAVY DEPARTMENT DEEPLY REGRETS TO INFORM YOU THAT YOUR

SONS WESLEY JOHN HEIDT FIREMAN FIRST CLASS US NAVY AND EDWARD

JOSEPH HEIDT FIREMAN FIRST CLASS US NAVY ARE MISSING FOLLOWING

ACTION IN THE PERFORMANCE OF THEIR DUTY AND IN THE SERVICE OF

THEIR COUNTRY X THE DEPARTMENT APPRECIATES YOUR GREAT ANXIETY AND

WILL FURNISH YOU FURTHER INFORMATION PROMPTLY WHEN RECEIVED X TO PREVENT

POSSIBLE AID TO OUR ENEMIES PLEASE DO NOT DIVULGE THE NAME OF THEIR

SHIP OR STATION

REAR ADMIRAL RANDALL JACOBS CHIEF OF THE BUREAU

OF NAVIGATION

1211A

These were the telegrams every family dreaded. Dispatched under the authority of the Secretary of War or of the Navy, the wires were sent to next of kin as soon as possible so that the terrible news wouldn't arrive first by radio or newspaper. Wesley and Edward Heidt were among three dozen pairs of brothers on the USS *Arizona*. Not a single pair survived intact. On November 22, 1941, Wesley had written his mother, "If anything happened to us, you would hear from the Navy the first thing." Opposite: The two red stars on the Western Union telegram would also have appeared on its envelope. They were a wartime signal to the carrier that the telegram contained news that was extremely sensitive to the recipient and accordingly should be delivered with appropriate care.

STANDARD TIME INDICATED

RECEIVED AT

TELEPHONE YOUR TELEGRAMS
TO POSTAL TELEGRAPH

Form 16A

Postal Telegraph

Mackay Radio

Commercial Cables

All America Cables

Canadian-Pacific Telegraphs

GRAM OR RADIOGRAM
INDICATED BY SYMBOL IN THE PREAMBLE
OR IN THE ADDRESS OF THE MESSAGE.
SYMBOLS DESIGNATING SERVICE SELECTED
ARE OUTLINED IN THE COMPANY'S TARIFFS
ON HAND AT EACH OFFICE AND ON FILE WITH
REGULATORY AUTHORITIES.

FB616 69 GOVT 6 EX CK US DELY OR OL CHGS

DX WASHINGTON DC 24 719P

1942 JAN 24 PM 6 31

MRS GENEVIEVE DUNLAP 1005

3545 LINDA VISTA TERRACE LOSA

AFTER EXHAUSTIVE SEARCH IT HAS BEEN FOUND IMPOSSIBLE TO LOCATE

YOUR SONS, WESLEY JOHN HEIDT FIREMAN FIRST CLASS US NAVY AND

EDWARD JOSEPH HEIDT FIREMAN FIRST CLASS US NAVY AND THEY

HAVE THEREFORE BEEN OFFICIALLY DECLARED TO HAVE LOST THEIR LIFE

IN THE SERVICE OF THEIR COUNTRY AS OF DECEMBER SEVENTH NINETEEN

FORTY ONE X THE DEPARTMENT EXPRESSES TO YOU ITS SINCEREST

SYMPATHY

REAR ADMIRAL RANDALL JACOBS CHIEF OF BUREAU OF NAVIGATION.

STANDARD TIME INDICATED

THIS IS A FULL RATE TELEGRAM, CABLE-

Following an ancient Hawaiian tradition, American sailors placed leis on the grave sites of their fallen comrades not far from the Kaneohe Naval Air Station. Losses sustained during the attack were stunning: 2,403 Americans were killed, another 1,178 wounded. Eighteen ships were sunk or seriously damaged, while 347 planes were destroyed or damaged. Had Nomura not ordered the Japanese ships to turn back before the third wave, these numbers would have been considerably higher.

National Archives

Meanwhile, in Washington, D.C., on that infamous date ...
By early evening, several hundred men, women and
children had gathered outside the White House—awaiting
word, keeping vigil, seeking some kind of communion.
Inside, the President was dictating a draft of the message
he would deliver to Congress asking for a declaration of
war. After a quiet dinner in his study, he went, at 8:30, to
the Oval Room to brief his Cabinet. There, he was blunt:
"The casualties, I am sorry to say, were extremely heavy."

Americans answered the bell in droves after the attack. At this New York City recruiting station, 18- and 19-year-olds were sworn in to the Army. Men who volunteered could pick their own branch of service.

Herbert Gehr

5 | THE CALL TO ARMS

Around the globe, reactions to the stunning attack on Pearl Harbor, and attempts to assess what would follow, could not have been more diverse. "We cannot lose the war!" said Adolf Hitler. "Now we have a partner who has not been defeated in three thousand years." The Free French leader Charles de Gaulle, in exile in England, also foresaw an ultimate result, but quite a different one. "The war is over," he said. "Of course there are years of fighting ahead, but the Germans are beaten." For his part, Adm. Yamamoto Isoroku, the architect of the Japanese attack, offered no firm predictions but observed ominously, "I fear all we have done is to awaken a sleeping giant and fill him with a terrible resolve."

The headline in LIFE was AMERICA GOES TO WAR, and the copy read, "In the nation's capital and in cities on both continental coasts the lights of peace flicked off. Troops in steel helmets bared bayonets before the gates of military establishments and areas of arms production. Enemy aliens—Japanese, Italians, Germans—were banged into prisons and detention camps. Interceptor planes stood ready and patrol planes roared ceaselessly along the shores of America's two oceans. Congress prepared to muster a gigantic pool of manpower—10,000,000 men between 19 and 45 for military service; 30,000,000 men up to 65 for defense activities of all kinds. The ban on overseas duty for selectees was lifted. Air-raid alarms sounded in Seattle, San Francisco, Los Angeles, New York. . . .At long last two-ocean war had come to America."

Formal declarations were hardly necessary, but in the week following the attack on Pearl Harbor they came fast—and furiously. For the record: On December 8, Japan and the U.S. exchanged pledges

The House of Representatives crackled with energy on December 8 when Franklin Delano Roosevelt delivered some of the most famous, and stirring, words in American history. The speech lasted only six minutes but would galvanize a nation. Within an hour, the U.S. was officially at war. Below: Roosevelt's revision of a first draft.

DRAFT No. 1

PROPOSED MESSAGE TO THE CONGRESS

December 7, 1941.

Yesterday, December 7, 1941, a date which will live in infamy

the United States of America was ~~suddenly~~ and deliberately attacked

by naval and air forces of the Empire of Japan

The United States was at the moment at peace with that nation and was still in conversations with its Government and its Emperor looking toward the maintenance of peace in the Pacific. Indeed, one hour after Japanese air squadrons had commenced bombing in Oahu the Japanese Ambassador to the United States and his colleague delivered to the Secretary of State a formal reply to a recent American message. This reply stated that it seemed useless to continue diplomatic negotiations, it contained no threat or hint of war or armed attack.

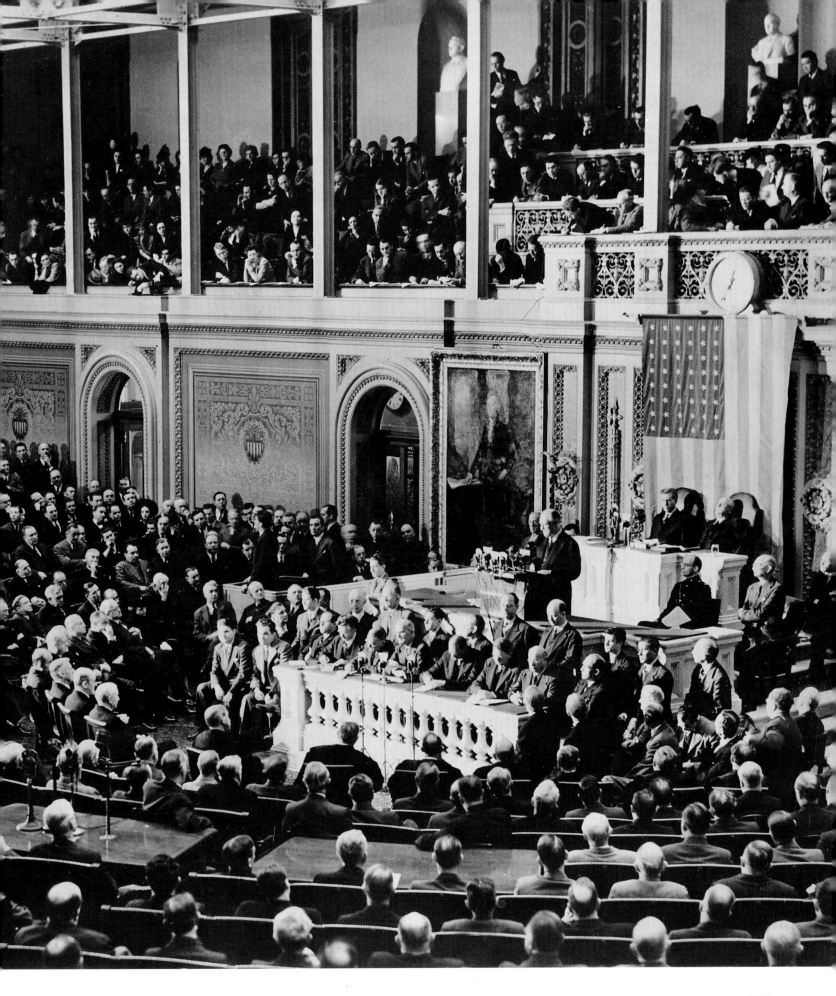

Any notion of American isolationism was obliterated by the news from Pearl Harbor. Even longtime critics of FDR knew that the man on the street was ready to take on the enemy. The headline of New York's *Daily Mirror* (right) captured the tenor of the day. Meanwhile, in Japan, the couple at left savored their news report of Japan's declaration of war.

to fight to the death. Three days later, Germany and Italy declared war on the U.S., which returned the favor by nightfall. "Last week war became worldwide," read the LIFE story. "Fighting in Europe, in Africa, in the Far East was merged into the same violent pattern. By week's end there were 33 nations involved, 25 on the side of the Allies, eight with the Axis." While statistically this was true, at the center of the conflict were Britain, the U.S.S.R. and the U.S. vs. Germany, Italy and Japan.

In the near term, Japanese successes in the Pacific augured ill for an Allied offensive in the East. Japan bombed the Philippines, Wake Island and Guam on December 8, while launching invasions of Thailand, Malaya and Hong Kong the same day. It invaded the Gilbert Islands on the 9th and Burma on the 11th. It invaded Borneo on the 16th and initiated a concerted offensive against the Philippines, defended by Gen. Douglas MacArthur's troops, on the 22nd. Japan captured Wake on the 23rd, and on Christmas, Hong Kong surrendered. Japan rang out 1941 with a New Year's Eve occupation of Manila, capital of the Philippines.

The United States was trying to mobilize, but the effort was proving difficult. America's giant industrial machine quickly went on a 24/7 schedule with a goal of a billion dollars in arms a week, but troops had to be trained, strategies formed. On December 10, U.S. aircraft sank a Japanese sub north of Oahu, and five days later a U.S. sub sank the Japanese merchant ship *Atsutasan Maru.* But such individual hits paled in comparison with Japan's dynamic expansion. On January 11, Japan invaded the Dutch East Indies. On the 20th, it pushed its offensive through Burma. On February 15, the crucial port of Singapore surrendered. In March, Japan entered the Burmese capital of Rangoon, accepted the surrender of Java and landed on the Solomon Islands. Meanwhile, MacArthur arrived in Australia from the Philippines, having promised to return—a pledge that appeared, at the time, optimistic.

If the U.S. war effort, particularly in the Pacific, was off to a wheel-spinning start, it wasn't for lack of spirit. Remember Pearl Harbor! was the overnight war cry of the American populace, and the press stopped speaking of "defense" in favor of "victory." The America First movement shuttered. A project conducted on December 8 on the streets of Washington, D.C., by the Library of Congress confirmed a pervasive stars-and-stripes mindset:

Archivist: How do you feel about this thing?

Man: Well … I didn't want us to go to war. I mean, like everyone else, we'd like to keep out of it. But now that we're in there, we go to work on them and really give them something … they'll be sorry for.

Archivist: How do you feel it's going to go?

Woman: I hope we beat the hell out of them … Our Air Force is strong enough to beat them all.

Archivist: Has the feeling of the people changed?

Man #2: Yes, they have.

Man #3: Yes, they have.

Man #4: Those who were against war now are for it. The everyday isolation has changed to an everyday defeat of Hitler, defeat of Nazism, or any '-ism' outside of Americanism.

So it went in Washington and elsewhere. In New York City, a young man grew impatient waiting in

Women worked alongside men in February 1942 on this assembly line in Cincinnati that made armor-piercing shells. As men shipped out, women stepped in, big-time: In 1941, they made up just 1 percent of all aviation employees; by 1943, they accounted for 65 percent. "Rosie the Riveter" had become vital.

the long line to enlist in the Army. He switched to the Navy line to hurry things along. A Bostonian named Mahoney pinned a note to the wall of the New Haven Railroad engine house where, until he did the pinning, he had been employed. "To my buddies at the roundhouse," Mahoney's note read. "The liberty we enjoy will never be destroyed while boys like you and I can prevent it. That is why I left my job here and enlisted in the United States Marines."

Such a willingness for a fight, bolstered by industrial might, would eventually turn all tides. In the Pacific theater, a shift came sooner than expected. It happened—it was allowed to happen—because the Japanese had made a crucial mistake.

They hadn't finished off Pearl Harbor.

Napoleon once observed, "To be defeated is pardonable; to be surprised—never!" The sentiment was strong among America's military brass in the days following the bombing. Admiral Kimmel clearly knew his fate even as the attack was in progress. He was standing by a window at Naval Command when a spent bullet shattered the glass, nicked him and fell to the floor. Kimmel picked up the slug and said, "It would have been merciful had it killed me."

He was relieved of his duties on December 17 and replaced as head of the Pacific Fleet by Rear Adm. Chester W. Nimitz. "I'm the new Commander in Chief," Nimitz, in evident distress, told his wife.

"You've wanted this all your life."

"But sweetheart," said Nimitz, "all the ships are at the bottom."

That wasn't quite so, and this made all the difference. As devoted as Yamamoto had been to the idea of a sneak attack, he was consistently reluctant to embrace any suggestion of a follow-up strike on Pearl. The Japanese had a golden opportunity to improve on their formal plans when Commander Fuchida, flush with success, implored Admiral Nagumo to okay a second mass aerial attack. Nagumo, knowing how Yamamoto felt and happy with the

Alfred T. Palmer/Library of Congress

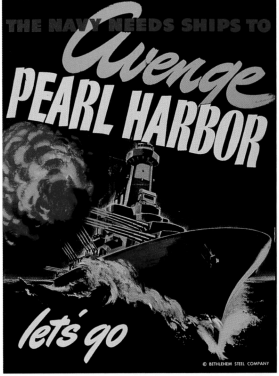

THE NAVY NEEDS SHIPS TO

Avenge

PEARL HARBOR

let's go

© BETHLEHEM STEEL COMPANY

In posters, speeches, movies and song, "Pearl Harbor" became synonymous with "sneak attack." Left: On March 1, 1942, the cruiser *Houston* was sunk by the Japanese, and all 1,068 aboard were killed or taken prisoner. Not long after, this plaza in Houston, Texas, was jammed for the swearing-in of Navy recruits who had enlisted to avenge the loss of the ship.

spoils won, said no. His carriers turned for Japan.

Vulnerable at Pearl Harbor were several damaged but not destroyed battleships, intact repair facilities and a massive cluster of oil tanks filled with fuel. Returning to Pearl from a mission to Wake Island was the USS *Enterprise,* which would have presented a prime target. That all of these assets were spared proved vital when, in early May 1942, the Japanese suffered setbacks during the Battle of the Coral Sea. Precisely a month later, the U.S. Pacific Fleet scored perhaps the greatest naval victory ever at the Battle of Midway, where it halted Japan's eastward push and let the Axis know that the fight was now well and truly engaged.

The Battle of Midway was the first major defeat suffered by the Japanese navy in 350 years. The results had a massive effect on the psychological profile of the war. What would end with atomic bombings began, of course, at Pearl Harbor. But it began again at Midway.

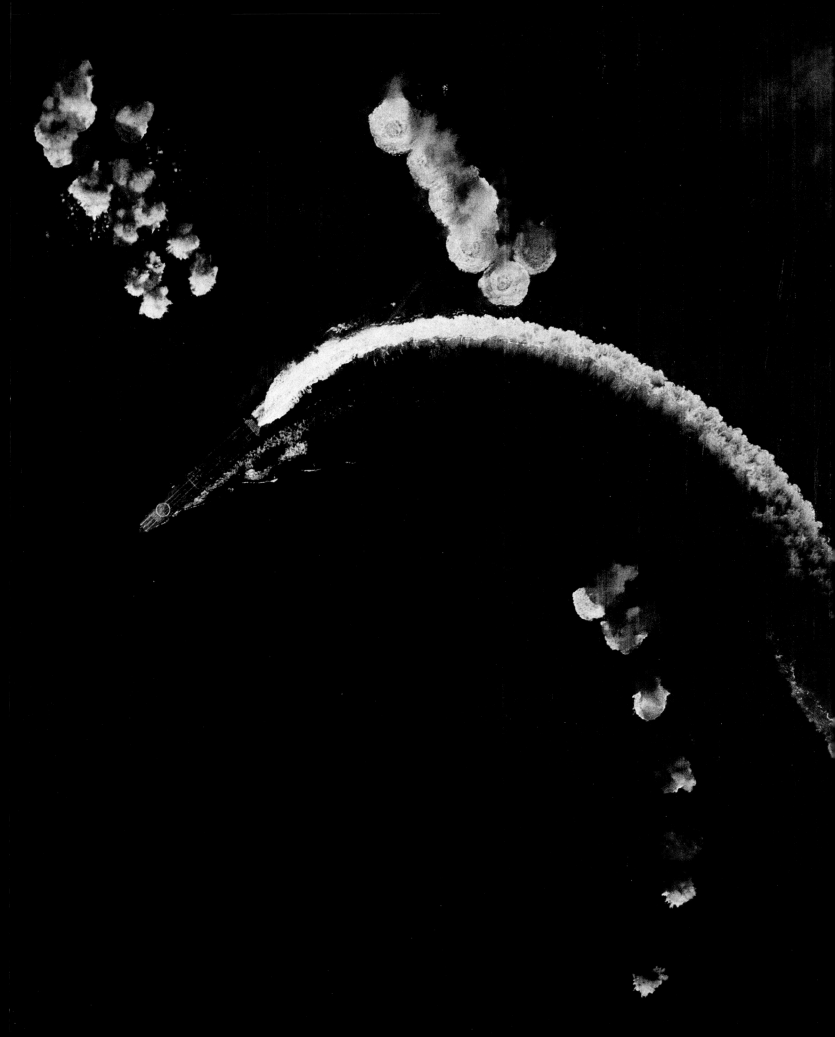

Payback came for the U.S. Navy in June 1942 with the Battle of Midway, at the western tip of the Hawaiian chain. Acting on intelligence reports, Adm. Chester W. Nimitz gathered ships that had survived Pearl Harbor and the Coral Sea, and ambushed the Japanese fleet. One U.S. carrier was sunk, but the Japanese navy was rocked by the loss of four carriers, all of which had participated at Pearl, including the *Hiryu,* seen at left trying to avoid high-level bombing. Above: These survivors of the *Hiryu* were picked up in a lifeboat two weeks later by the *Ballard.* Below: "Dauntless" dive-bombers from the *Hornet* approached the burning cruiser *Mikuma.*

The *West Virginia* was struck by two bombs and at least seven torpedoes, resulting in tremendous damage to her port side (opposite, looking aft, in dry dock at the Navy Yard at Pearl). The ship was out of commission until July 1944 but later that year played a vital role at the Battle of Surigao Strait, in the Philippines. (It was the last time battleships would square off—in any war, anywhere.) The "Wee Vee" went on to wield her big guns in operations at Iwo Jima and Okinawa, and was in Tokyo Bay for the formal Japanese surrender. Above and right: There was never serious hope that the *Arizona* could be revived, although there had been some thought given to salvaging the relatively intact after portion. With work from the likes of these divers, most of the ship's guns were recovered and many were put back into service.

These pictures show three stages in the herculean effort to right and refloat the capsized *Oklahoma*. Returning the ship to action was never a real consideration; rather, this was a matter of clearing an important berth at the port, which would continue to play a major staging role in the war. The Japanese decision to forgo a final attack wave was a critical error. Oil tanks containing 4.5 million barrels of precious fuel were sitting ducks. Without those tanks, the Pacific Fleet would have been forced back to the West Coast, seriously retarding offensive operations.

On April 19, 1942, the *Nevada* prepared to steam to Puget Sound for further repairs and modernization. The only battleship to get under way during the attack at Pearl, she returned to combat in May 1943 and took part in many major operations. From the months and years that followed Pearl Harbor and Midway, the annals of the war in the Pacific ring with names that will stir souls forever: Tarawa ... Guadalcanal ... the Gilbert, Marshall and Mariana islands ... New Guinea ... Saipan ... Burma ... Leyte Gulf ... Iwo Jima ... Okinawa ... ending at last on September 2, 1945, with the formal Japanese surrender aboard the USS *Missouri*.

PH2c H.S. Fawcett, USN

In the Manzanar camp, three young detainees were posed at a barbed wire fence by fellow inmate Toyo Miyatake, a Los Angeles photographer who had fashioned a wooden camera out of a lens and film holder that he had sneaked past the guards.

THE "ENEMY" WITHIN

Toyo Miyatake

The fallout from the attack was immediate and multifaceted. As **Charles Hirshberg** writes, one manifestation—the internment of innocent Japanese-Americans—was more than unfortunate. It was ugly.

Within 12 hours of the attack across the Pacific in Hawaii, it seemed as though a bomb had fallen on Yoshiko Uchida's Northern California home. "A strange man sat in our living room," Uchida would later recall, "and my father was gone."

It would have been hard to imagine a family more innocuous than the Uchidas. Yoshiko's mother, Iku, kept house, cooked scrumptious sukiyaki and, as a hobby, collected dolls. Her father, Dwight, an assistant manager at an import-export firm, grew white chrysanthemums and prizewinning gladiolas in the front yard. Yoshiko was a senior at the University of California at Berkeley, an American citizen who had grown up drinking from a Little Orphan Annie mug and romping around Alameda county with her collie, Laddie.

Nonetheless, on December 7, 1941, the Uchidas were declared enemies of the United States, and so Dwight was led away while the "strange man"— an FBI agent—continued to guard Iku and Yoshiko. Within months, the rest of the family would be ushered to an assembly center at the Tanforan Race Track in San Bruno, Calif., for assignment to one of 10 camps—prisons— designed to house Japanese-Americans during the war. Years later Yoshiko would still remember their quarters at Tanforan: a horse stall that stank of manure. It had been hastily whitewashed; crumpled corpses of spiders were stuck to the walls.

It happened with stunning speed for the Uchidas and very fast for most Japanese-Americans. With the attack on Pearl Harbor, many male non-citizens who had been born in Japan, like Dwight Uchida, were immediately rounded up, and calls for the imprisonment of everyone with Japanese blood—U.S. citizen or not—were instantly in the air. Secretary of the Navy Frank Knox, desperately trying to shift the blame for the disaster at Pearl Harbor, led the call for lockup, insisting that an "effective fifth column" of Japanese-Americans had somehow aided the Japanese attack. The fever spread. "Herd 'em up, pack 'em off and give 'em the inside room in the badlands," wrote Henry McLemore in his Hearst-chain column. "Let 'em be pinched, hurt, hungry and dead up against it … And that goes for all of them." While some level-headed government officials pleaded for calm, others pressed for action, both to stem espionage activities that Japanese-Americans might be engaged in and to protect them from the worst impulses of their neighbors. California congressman Leland Ford, whose state was home to

National Archives

the great majority of the nation's 127,000 Japanese-Americans, telephoned the U.S. Attorney General's office and, as Ford later recalled, "I told them to stop f---ing around. I gave them twenty four hours' notice that unless they would issue a mass evacuation notice I would … give the bastards everything [I] could with both barrels."

On February 19, 1942, Roosevelt signed Executive Order 9066, a law enabling the eventual "relocation" to other states or to internment camps of 120,000 West Coast Japanese-Americans, citizens and resident aliens alike. The presumption was that those nearest the Pacific would be of most use to the Japanese military, and should therefore be moved inland.

The detainees were instructed to bring only what they could carry to one of 16 assembly centers—compounds thrown together at fairgrounds, racetracks, even a stockyard in Portland, Ore. The prisoners traveled in a daze, surrounded by armed military guards. William Marutani, then a student at the University of Washington, was so stunned that he blanked out completely. "I literally

Above: In April 1942, a young girl waited to be bused to an assembly center for relocation. Right: That same month, a train packed with Japanese-Americans from San Pedro, Calif., arrived at the Santa Anita center, the system's largest, which at one point housed 18,719 on the grounds of an erstwhile racetrack.

don't remember the trip," he says 59 years later. "I formed a mental block and just shut down." "It had never occurred to us that we might be picked up," says George Aratani, who was, at the time, a 24-year-old produce supplier in the Santa Maria Valley in California. "We were Americans." Aratani decided to try to retain ownership of his company during his detention, but many other businessmen sold out hastily, usually for a pittance. Possessions, too, were sold or forfeited. A white woman stopped by the Uchidas' house and asked if she might dig up Dwight's gladiolas. "Since you're leaving anyway," the woman offered helpfully.

The first camp to open was Manzanar, and with its eventual population of 10,000 it became, for a time, the largest city between L.A. and Reno. The

Clem Albers/National Archives

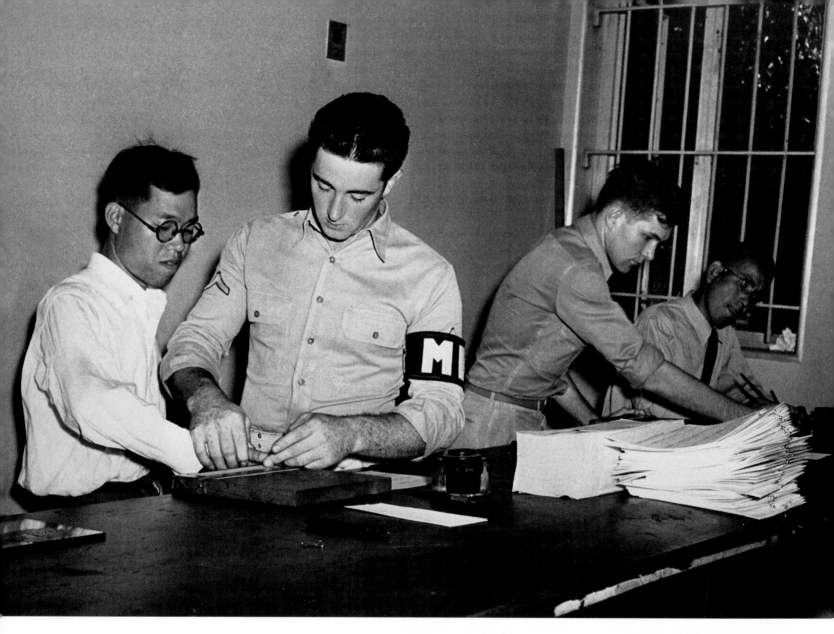

Uchidas were sent from Tanforan to the Topaz camp in Utah. In February, 12 members of the Miyahara family were processed at Tanforan for transport to the Topaz camp as well. Flo Miyahara, 18 at the time, still remembers the experience vividly: her large family jammed into two rooms of a tar-paper shack at the racetrack. Flo was told to fill a sack with straw; this would be her new bed. She did so, then went outside and walked to the fence that surrounded Tanforan. "I couldn't believe where I was," she says now. "I just stood there staring at the road, watching the cars drive by. All my life, I had been free to go where I wanted; now I wasn't, and I just couldn't understand why. I couldn't stop watching the cars. After many hours, my family had to actually pry my fingers from the fence."

George Aratani was sent out of state. "The windows on the train were closed and the shades

were drawn," he remembers. "We were told not to look out, but we were curious. Whenever someone tried to peek through, a soldier would shout, 'Hey, you! Keep away from that window!'" When the train finally halted, Aratani was shocked to find himself in the Arizona desert. Two camps, which together would eventually house 15,000, had been built on the Gila River Indian Reservation; overcrowding was the order of the day, with as many as 25 people living in a space designed for four.

Bob Sakata was 16 when he arrived at the similarly desolate and crowded Topaz camp. He was trying to believe that he was being relocated in part for his own safety. But one look at the camp guards and he knew it was a lie: "I thought, if they're here to protect us, their guns should be pointing out, away from us. But they weren't."

By October 1942, 100,000 detainees were living in 10 camps scattered throughout the West. Most compounds were surrounded by barbed wire, watchtowers and sentries. By design, the locations of the camps were remote; most were in the desert, where the climate was harsh. Wind would whip dust through cracks in the walls of the crude barracks. Preserving food in this environment was difficult, and illness spread. Almost no preparation had been made by authorities to provide for the health of the prisoners, or to educate the thousands of children now under guard.

The inmates, therefore, shouldered new responsibilities. Those with training in first aid became nurses. The college-educated, like Yoshiko Uchida, became school teachers. At first, classes were held without the benefit of desks or chairs. Yoshiko remembered snakes slithering in from the desert and having to send children home in tempests of dust: a very different kind of snow day.

In many camps, students dutifully began each day with the Pledge of Allegiance, followed by a chorus of "My Country, 'Tis of Thee." "There was a terrible combination of concern and depression, but my father was always telling us: Try to prove you're worthy of being in this country," says Sakata.

As he implies, the psychological wounds inflicted on the prisoners ran deeper than any physical effects of their depredation. Though they had done no wrong, many began to blame themselves. "America was our mother, the only mother we had," explains William Marutani, who was

AP/Wide World

Opposite: Detainees were fingerprinted in Honolulu in February 1942. In March, new arrivals at Manzanar made beds of straw. Many at Manzanar were from L.A., including all members of the Chick-a-dee Japanese Girls Softball Team, who kept in practice (above). In a graduation wish to the class of '42, Ralph Merritt, the official who ran the camp, wrote: "I hope you may say that Manzanar was a wartime city ... where students dedicated their future lives to the American way of living."

imprisoned at Tule Lake, Calif., until he succeeded in joining the Army in 1944. "You start to think, 'If my mother's doing this to me, she must have a damn good reason.'"

"Hardest hit were the women," says Cherry Tsutsumida, who spent three years of her childhood in a camp on the Gila River. "I used to hear them crying at night. Mothers had no idea what was going on: What had they done wrong? I was nine, and these women would ask me to teach them to read English, so they could understand things better. They were too embarrassed to ask the older kids, so we'd sit and read my little book.

"It was like being raped, and then being treated like everything that happened was your fault. You began to feel ashamed."

One day, Flo Miyahara snapped at her mother: "You shouldn't have had children! Then we wouldn't be here!" Not long after, Flo and some friends made a pathetic attempt to escape. They got as far as a local train station before they were caught by soldiers. "One was named Lieutenant Nails. He kicked one of our guys and said, 'If you move, I'll blow a hole in you as big as a barn.'" Some prisoners actually were shot, including Shoichi James Okamoto of Garden Grove, Calif., who was killed during an altercation with a sentry at the Tule Lake camp in California; James Hatsuki Wakasa, who reportedly tried to escape from the

The camps differed in size but not in design: "blocks" consisting of 12 barracks, perhaps half a dozen rooms per barrack, about 400 square feet each and housing at least one family per room. The Hosokawas dressed up their quarters at the Heart Mountain Relocation Center in northwestern Wyoming as best they could.

Hansel Mieth

Manzanar camp; and at least half a dozen others. An Army officer at Manzanar reported to an official that sentries "were finding guard service very monotonous, and that nothing would suit them better than to have a little excitement, such as shooting a Jap."

The most vicious attitudes began to change as the war went on and the public came to realize that the detainees were not a threat to the nation. Not least, thousands of Japanese-Americans were buying credibility by performing nobly in the armed services. Twenty-five thousand Japanese-Americans volunteered for duty in World War II; 4,000 of them came from the camps. In the fall of 1943, the 100th Battalion, a Hawaiian national guard unit composed of ethnic Japanese, served so heroically in the Italian campaign that it became known as the Purple Heart Battalion. The 442nd Regimental Combat Team—made up in great measure of men recruited from the camps—became one of the most decorated units in the U.S. military, garnering a Congressional Medal of Honor, 47 Distinguished Service Crosses, 350 Silver Stars, 810 Bronze Stars and more than 3,600 Purple Hearts. President Truman would later congratulate these soldiers for fighting against "not only the enemy, but prejudice."

Beginning in 1943, some prisoners were quietly discharged from the camps. In June 1944, Interior Secretary Harold Ickes advised President Roosevelt that "the continued retention of these innocent people ... would be a blot upon the history of this country." With an upcoming election, Roosevelt demurred "for the sake of internal quiet." However, on December 17, 1944, with FDR's reelection a fait accompli, a public proclamation was issued declaring that the government had "carefully examined" more than 115,000 Japanese-Americans—including 20,000 under age 14—and had concluded that they should be "allowed to enjoy the same privileges accorded other law-abiding American citizens or residents."

At the relocation center in Heart Mountain, Wyo., some of the 12,000 Japanese-American internees saluted their country's flag in -18° weather. The camp foreman, noting cracks in the walls of the ramshackle barracks, said, "Well, I guess those Japs will be stuffing their underwear in there to keep the wind out."

Hansel Mieth

One of the most ignoble chapters in America's wartime history was ended.

For all former detainees, the nightmare would linger as they made their way in a society that had treated them harshly. William Marutani became a judge in Philadelphia. Dr. Flo Miyahara devoted her life to pediatric medicine in Denver. Bob Sakata, also of Denver, was a farmer. Cherry Tsutsumida worked for Senator Ted Kennedy's office as a Congressional Fellow. George Aratani, who lives in Los Angeles, founded two corporations: Mikasa, the dinnerware and crystal company, and Kenwood, the electronics giant. All remain vital as the 60th anniversary of their incarceration nears.

Yoshiko Uchida became an author. Before her death in 1992, she wrote numerous charming children's books, such as *The Dancing Kettle* and *Two Foolish Cats*. She also wrote *The Invisible Thread*, which is based in part on her experiences at the Utah compound.

In 1983, the Commission on Wartime Relocation and Internment of Civilians, having conducted an investigation, recommended that Congress make reparations to those who spent time in the camps. Five years later, America officially apologized for its actions. In 1990, Congress started to pay $1.25 billion to still-living survivors. And this year—on June 29, 2001—the National Japanese American Memorial to Patriotism opens in Washington, D.C. A bronze statue depicts two 14-foot cranes, wings spread as they free themselves from a tangle of barbed wire. Inscribed on the wall behind it is a history of Japanese-Americans in wartime, as well as the names of soldiers who died in World War II—a war during which, it is interesting to note, not a single known act of espionage was committed by a Japanese-American.

George Aratani, now 84, is asked if he remains as patriotic as ever. "Sure," he replies, a little surprised by the question. "Why not? Just because the United States kicked us around doesn't make us any less American."

Pearl Harbor 2001
Jerry Bruckheimer and Michael Bay's costly (the budget of $130-million-plus was the biggest ever green-lighted) extravaganza relies heavily on special effects and location shooting. When the film was originally announced, the title was *Tennessee,* after the battleship.

Photofest (2)

7 | BOMBS AND SMASHES

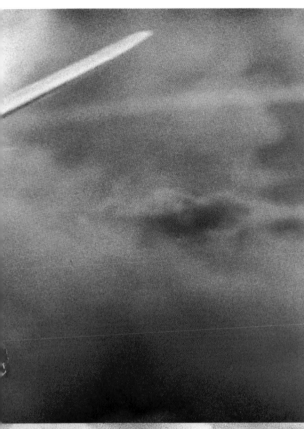

Nowhere has Pearl Harbor lived in infamy—and tragedy and treachery and love and lust—as it has on screen, writes **Richard Schickel.** The latest version proves the point again—pumping up the volume.

Pearl Harbor is one of the ghosts haunting our collective memory—cautionary symbol, hinge of fate, continuing enigma. It is something like the sinking of the *Titanic* in that it appears to have been a preventable disaster—if only its victims had recognized the signs hinting at impending catastrophe. It is something like the assassination of John F. Kennedy in that we search for conspiracies dark and grand enough in design to match the magnitude of the crime. It is like all great calamities in that, if we were alive when they occurred, we never forget where we were when we heard the news, never quite escape our stunned incomprehension as the early bulletins coalesced into the primitive draft of a typical modernist narrative—innocence betrayed, historical coherence shattered, peaceful expectations violated.

One of the curiosities about such events is that they elude art. There have been, up till recently, no great fictions in print or on screen about them. In that sense, Pearl Harbor is typical; in the years since the Japanese planes shattered the peace of that December Sunday morning, it has yet to tempt any writer or filmmaker of true eminence. It is a Battle of Borodino awaiting its Tolstoy, an Aqaba looking for its David Lean. Mostly, it has been a subject for historians, who have kept asking: What did they know and when did they know it? They have spent the past 60 years disputing whether President Roosevelt and his top aides knew the attack was coming and, if they did, why they did not more urgently alert their troops.

That's a side issue for Michael Bay and Jerry Bruckheimer, respectively the director and producer of the new film *Pearl Harbor.* Some 45 minutes of their movie is devoted to the attack itself, but that's—literally—not the half of it. More screen time is spent on an entirely fictional romantic triangle—two hot pilots (Ben Affleck and Josh Hartnett) in love with a Navy nurse (Kate Beckinsale). Before Pearl Harbor, Affleck's character sees action with the Eagle Squadron, composed of American recruits who fought in the Battle of Britain. Afterward, both aviators fly on the Doolittle raid against Japan, which five months after Pearl Harbor exacted our first revenge against the Japanese homeland.

Pearl Harbor is a spectacular orchestration of special effects. Bay and Bruckheimer are acutely conscious of the fact that, because of the costs involved—not to mention the alarming decline in the public's historical

Air Force 1943

Directed by Howard Hawks and written by Dudley Nichols, this exciting film was a classic of the different-sorts-of-Joes-*can*-work-together genre. The solid cast was led by John Garfield as a cynical tail gunner.

consciousness—this is probably the last time this battle will be represented on the screen. Their account is loaded with true anecdotes about the attack, gathered from close to a hundred interviews with survivors. Typical is a low-flying Japanese pilot trying to wave away some kids playing baseball, warning them to take cover before the bombs begin falling.

On the other hand, they are forthright about the fact that their film follows the *Titanic* model, foregrounding an entirely fictional love story. They need the female audience that is generally turned off by war movies. As Bay coolly says of James Cameron's megahit, "without the love story, all you have is a sinking ship." Bay has a lot more of them, obviously, but that's not necessarily an advantage in attracting the vast audience he needs.

Nor is this necessarily a new idea. There have

been a dozen American movies that have significantly dealt with Pearl Harbor, only two of which have focused exclusively on it. The rest have done what Bay is doing—touched upon it and then moved on to something more inspirational.

This strategy was pioneered by director Howard Hawks, whose *Air Force* appeared barely a year after the attack. It is about the flight of B-17s that takes off from California for Oahu's Hickam Field on December 6, 1941, and flies right into World War II the next morning. Interestingly, that mission is historically true, and because its anticipated arrival time coincided with the Japanese attack, it helped lull the island's defenders. Radar operators were assured that those mysterious blips on their screen were friendlies.

The B-17s in *Air Force* were armed—which was

Through Tokyo's Lens

The Japanese did not fight the war for their right to boo the Honshu Dodgers. Or for Mom's rice cakes. Their propaganda stressed a subordination of self to the demands of a near-feudal state.

The three Japanese films that deal significantly with the attack on Pearl Harbor all feature naval cadets who are taught this hard warrior's code as boys, and then, as young officers, demonstrate their willingness to die for it. **The War at Sea from Hawaii to Malaya** (1942) offers a spectacular special-effects sequence that re-creates the assault on Pearl. But its big climax occurs when the pilot of a crippled plane impresses his squadron (and presumably the audience) by turning himself into a kamikaze and crashing suicidally into a U.S. ship.

I Bombed Pearl Harbor (1962) and **Imperial Navy** (1981) take the story further—to the decisive Japanese defeat at Midway. The former lets its hero live; the latter shows two brothers dying heroically. Neither, however, questions the morality of the sneak attack (Admiral Yamamoto is portrayed as a man doing a somewhat distasteful duty). Both

films insist that the outnumbered Americans won at Midway not because of superior fighting skills but because, having cracked the Japanese code, they had a huge intelligence advantage. Finally, both are insanely dull movies, interesting only as they glancingly, belatedly, question the cruel militarism that led Japan to disaster.

Above: *I Bombed Pearl Harbor* featured Toshiro Mifune (left). Below: A miniature of Battleship Row was created for *The War at Sea from Hawaii to Malaya.*

not true of the historical bombers headed for the Pacific—and when they landed they were told most of the damage at Hickam was the result of sabotage, which was then a common and entirely false rumor. But these discrepancies aside, *Air Force* is a better-than-average war movie, full of understated heroism as the socially disparate crew of the featured bomber, the *Mary Ann,* bonds under pressure and becomes an efficient fighting machine. But the plane is on the ground in Hawaii only long enough to refuel and rearm. Then it is up and buzzing steadily westward—to Wake Island, the Philippines, eventually to what appears to be the Battle of the Coral Sea, seeking participation in a heartening American victory.

Pearl Harbor was alluded to in dozens of American wartime movies—with contempt for the sneakiness of the Japanese, with high resolve about recovering from the blow. *Air Force* was the only one that depicted some of the devastation. In the postwar era, those few movies that touched on the topic—*Task Force, In Harm's Way, Midway*—followed the *Air Force* model. We would see a low-flying Zero strafe an innocent or two. Cut to a general or admiral assessing the damage. Join Gary Cooper or John Wayne putting out to sea, looking for a compensatory victory.

The notable exception is director Fred Zinnemann's fine 1953 adaptation of the famous James Jones novel *From Here to Eternity.* It captures, better than any other movie, the irrational panic of the

From Here to Eternity 1953

A powerful piece of American filmmaking, Fred Zinnemann's *Eternity* copped eight Oscars (tying 1939's *Gone With the Wind*), including Best Picture. The no-nonsense portrayal of Army life before and after the attack was intensified by the against-the-grain casting of Deborah Kerr, Donna Reed and, of course, Frank Sinatra, in his legendary comeback role. Below: Kerr and Burt Lancaster, memorably, on the shore.

The Everett Collection

Photofest

populace after the attack. Montgomery Clift portrays Robert E. Lee Prewitt as a knothead who is hurt and AWOL following a (justifiable) homicide. But Prewitt is also an Army lifer, a 30-year man whose only home is the military. Now that war has so shockingly broken out, he must rejoin his unit, whatever the consequences. Attempting to do so, he is shot by a patrol nervously on the alert for those mythical saboteurs.

It is one of the movies' most poignant representations of the self-destructiveness often inherent in dutifulness. But it is also a bummer placed atop a bigger historical bummer, and you can see why no one has come close to imitating it. If death is inevitable in war movies, we want it to be heroic, not absurdist; altruistic, not ironic.

This does not mean, however, that we want the hysterical didacticism of the first movie to devote itself to Pearl Harbor, the unreleased *December 7th,* or the determined factuality of the other, 1970's *Tora! Tora! Tora!* Behind the former lies a fascinating story. Produced by director John Ford's Field Photographic Service, a branch of the OSS, it was directed by Gregg Toland, the great cinematographer of *Citizen Kane.* He and a crew were at Pearl when the wreckage was still smoking. Since there were no more than a couple of minutes of authentic footage of the attack, Toland set about re-creating it: An outdoor church service is interrupted by the Japanese planes; real sailors, pressed into service by Toland, run around impotently shooting machine guns and dying like Hollywood extras.

But that wasn't enough for him. He conceived a loopy parable in which Uncle Sam (played by Walter Huston) is discovered taking a sleepy Hawaiian vacation while little brown men skulk about—peering through cane fields to note ship traffic, listening outside the men's room door as American officers carelessly discuss military secrets. Uncle Sam's conscience (Harry Davenport) keeps trying to warn him about this skulduggery, but he's having too much hedonistic fun. It's not until the model ships are blowing up in the harbor that he pays attention. Toland enlisted the 20th Century Fox special-effects department, as well as a lot of other prominent players of the time

(Dana Andrews, William Demarest), to build his "documentary" to feature length.

It appalled the Pentagon. Even at a time when thousands of loyal Japanese-Americans were being shipped off to internment camps, the film's racist lunacy was judged detrimental to "national unity." Ford stepped in, reducing the film to 34 minutes, cutting all fictional elements, stressing the salvage of ships damaged in the attack so they could fight again, and released his version as a morale builder. Still containing Toland's toy ships and planes, it actually won an Oscar for best documentary in 1943. The longer, madder version languished in film archives for four decades before being released on home video.

Tora! Tora! Tora! 1970

Utilizing Japanese directors (Kinji Fukasaku and Toshio Masuda) along with American Richard Fleischer, this film was painstaking in its effort to be accurate. At times, though, attempts to avoid offending anyone led to strained, tepid scenes. Still, it is engrossing, and wisely drew heavily from the work of Pearl Harbor historian Gordon W. Prange. Admiral Kimmel was played by Martin Balsam, and General Short by Jason Robards. George Macready provided a stoic Cordell Hull.

Tora! Tora! Tora! (1970) is *December 7th*'s diametric opposite, a relentlessly sober, extraordinarily truthful docudrama, devoting perhaps a third of its running time to the attack. Another third of it shows the Japanese planning the assault. They speak in their native tongue and are represented, non-pejoratively, as military men going professionally about their business. The remaining strand offers American intelligence officers hunching over their decoding devices and trying fecklessly to get their commanders to heed their suspicions. *Tora! Tora! Tora!* was both a huge flop and, just possibly, the most historically accurate feature film ever made. With its stern avoidance of romance, of overt villainy and hyped heroism, it may be also be a cinematic gesture as nutty as Toland's. Imagine thinking the inherent drama of a huge historical event could hold people's attention without the interpolation of doomed romance and period songs.

Bay and Bruckheimer rely on such disarming effects. They also seem to feel that we are finally so far away from the date that was supposed to live in infamy that we can regard it with a certain measure of equanimity. Once, Pearl Harbor very usefully made our patriotic blood boil; now, possibly we can see it as a nostalgic—even romantic—footnote in the annals of human folly. In other words, in the moviemakers' calculation, Pearl Harbor is, like the *Titanic,* perfectly ripe for Hollywood.

Victor Delano
Ensign, USS *West Virginia*

" The torpedoes demolished the whole side of the ship. We could hear the people on the other side of the water-tight bulkheads. They were scream-ing. There was nothing that we could do.

By the time I got topside, the whole port side of the ship was smashed in. There were fires. The *West Virginia* for a long time had bragged about being the smartest battleship in the fleet. Now here was the ship just completely in shambles.

Captain Bennion had just been severely wounded—hit by shrapnel that had ripped his whole interior. I was told to do whatever I could for him. I got him to a better spot. I got a first-aid kit. They were supposed to have morphine in it, but that was a drug and we weren't at war, so they hadn't authorized the morphine. I soaked a cloth in ether and tried to make him more comfortable.

Then Lieutenant Ricketts arrived. He was the one who saved the ship from rolling over. He went below and counterflooded. If he hadn't done that, we could have rolled over just the way the *Oklahoma* did.

I remember seeing the second wave. I must have been up there when the *Arizona* blew up. I saw other harbor activity. I saw the *Nevada* get under way and go by, and it got attacked and went aground.

I got two machine guns operating. An officer and two enlisted men arrived, and I assigned them to these guns and showed them how to operate them. The second wave was mainly horizontal bombers, up too high to be bothered by any .50-caliber machine guns. But the gunners didn't know that. They were feeling pretty deadly about this thing. The guns then jammed and they left.

Soon after that the smoke got so heavy that I had to get off the bridge. I couldn't even see where I was going. I moved in the direction of Turret No. 2. I jumped to the top of Turret No. 1 and then came down the side of it and got on the main deck and carefully took off my uniform and folded it.

I took my shoes off and started to swim toward the *Maryland*. Just as I started, fire broke out on the water ahead of me. So I tried to get to the *Tennessee*. There were oil slicks, some of which would ignite. I was just trying to keep away from whatever oil I could keep away from. There was an old chief petty officer, and I heard his voice behind saying, 'Help, save me, I can't swim!' I was physically really in no condition to help anybody, so I thought I'd say some-thing nice to him. So as I turned to encourage him, he went sailing past me on the water, still saying, 'Help, save me, I can't swim!' I finally gave up and swam ashore to Ford Island.

In the afternoon I went back to the *West Virginia* to help in fire fighting. I put on a gas mask in order to work in the smoke. At some point there was some kind of an explosion. Next thing I knew, I was put in a boat along with an enlisted man. The two of us were taken over to the Submarine Base hospital. I was there overnight. The hospital then said, 'If you want to go, you can go.' So I left. I was wrapped in a sheet, and went to the Submarine Base Navy Exchange to get a uniform. "

Delano was the son of a Navy captain and a distant cousin of President Franklin D. Roosevelt. He later commanded a destroyer during the Korean war and worked stateside during the Vietnam conflict. At 81, the retired captain lives in Maryland.

Bill Frakes for LIFE

They were at Pearl Harbor on December 7, 1941. Now, in interviews 60 years after the attack, these survivors remember that fateful day.

Abe was 21 when he graduated from Japan's Naval Academy in 1937. Pearl Harbor was his first attack mission. He continued flying throughout the war until stranded in the Mariana Islands in June 1944. After the war he was a colonel in the Japan Self-Defense Force. At 85, he is retired in Koganei.

Abe Zenji
Dive-bomber Pilot, *Akagi*

" One day in October 1941, an officer took the curtain off a table to reveal to us a model of Pearl Harbor. 'All of you are wondering what is going on,' he said. 'For the last four months, we've been doing different training. If we don't tell you why, it could affect your fighting spirit. Japan has been negotiating with the U.S. patiently to maintain our position in East Asia. But the U.S. doesn't seem willing to compromise. The relationship is getting worse. So we might have to attack Pearl Harbor in the near future.' It was the secret of all secrets.

Some of us felt like a cloud covering the sky had now been cleared up and there was a target to go for. I knew America must be a quite big and wealthy country. But on the other hand, we were directly descended from the gods, while Americans were people gathered from all over the world, a country of only 200 years. So they shouldn't have our fighting spirit. I didn't feel any fear.

I was a squadron leader on the *Akagi*. Before I set off, I changed my old underwear to my new ones. I put on my best uniform, my flying uniform, the khaki-colored one. Every aircraft carrier had a shrine. I went underneath and prayed at the shrine. I bowed just once. 'I am going now,' I said.

When the first group left, before dawn, it was dark. As the aircraft went off, they had their lights on, and it was like the sky was filled with fireflies. It was a beautiful scene—183 aircraft in the dark sky. It was the most beautiful thing I had ever seen.

It was getting brighter. I was at the back of the second fleet. There were 70 dive-bombers in the group. If you are flying, following another aircraft, the propeller engine makes a smoke stream, so to avoid it I was flying a little bit higher than the aircraft in front of me. I was near the end of the second group. The leader was at 3,000 meters. Each of the other planes was a little bit higher. I was at 3,500 meters. I felt like a shepherd watching the flock. I felt good about that.

I could see 200 to 300 bombs exploding on the ground. I immediately thought that the first group must be under counterattack from the Americans. From the sky, it was hard to distinguish the ships. I could see a huge ship, so I attacked. I learned later that it was the *Arizona,* already sinking. But it was my first mission; I just concentrated on what I was going to attack—I didn't think anything. There were lots of guns firing at me. I concentrated on my target.

I went to the Arizona Memorial recently and looked underneath. Every 40 seconds a bubble comes up. There are 1,177 dead buried there. I felt like those bubbles coming up were the bubbles of resentment of those dead. And I regret that. I shed a tear. Why Americans feel anger toward Japan— why they still hate us—I understand.

The most shameful thing is what I found out later. I found out that the Japanese government didn't declare war until after the attack. And even after we found out that the declaration of war had been delayed, no one apologized. **"**

Anna Busby
Lieutenant, Army Nurse Corps

"I went to Hawaii in June 1941. I was a second lieutenant in the Army Nurse Corps, assigned to Tripler Hospital in Honolulu. On December 7, when the Japanese attacked at five minutes to eight, I was actually staying in the hospital as a patient, ambulatory with an infected right cheek.

I remember that the head nurse ran down the hall, which was very unusual, to the back lanai on the second floor—the women's ward. I ran after her. What I saw then was the enormous smoke and fire from Hickam Field and Pearl Harbor. *Boom-boom-boom-boom-boom!* To our left, something hit the pineapple cannery, and that went up in a huge fire. I was petrified.

The head nurse picked up a phone and called Hickam, then said, 'My God, the Japanese are bombing Pearl Harbor!' I picked up my little radio and record player and hurried outside. About a hundred feet from the nurses' quarters, I ran into a nurse who carried a picnic basket on her arm. She said, 'Anna, we're going on a picnic to celebrate my boyfriend's birthday,' which is the sort of thing that we did on Sundays. I said, 'No one's going anywhere. We will all be needed on duty.'

After that I went to the chief nurse. Well, she took one look at me and said, 'Where do you think you're going with that red face? You look like a casualty.' She then ordered me to take care of the women's ward.

There were many patients there already, and then the injured started coming. By 9 a.m., the two lanais were both filled with casualties on litters. These were the very, very injured ones. I wasn't in the ward long when a patient shouted, 'Nurse, there's a fire down here.' I ran to the room that she was pointing at, and there was this beautiful, elderly woman, all made up—she looked just like a Dresden doll. She had been smoking and her handkerchief on the enamel table had caught on fire. I picked up her cigarettes and threw them in the drawer. I told her sternly, 'I don't have time to stay with you.'

I was truly busy for days. The only thing I can say is, the whole time, I was petrified. When the night nurse came on at 7 p.m. to relieve me on that first day, I was actually too scared to go back to my quarters. I was afraid that I wouldn't be able to speak if the sentry said, 'Halt. Who goes there?' I didn't know if I could answer. So I ended up staying at the hospital.

The next morning, December 8, at 6 a.m., the night nurse and I were standing out on the front lanai. We were sure that we heard a plane fly over the hospital and fire on the roof of the dental clinic. I have no idea if anyone was hurt. I was concerned with carrying out my duties on the women's ward, and that was it."

Busby, 89, resides in Montgomery, Ala. Since 1969, she has served as the National Chairlady of the White Caps, which is an organization of Army and Navy nurses who served on Oahu during the attack. Busby hopes to be able to publish an autobiography in the near future. One title that she is considering is *Wherever You Need Me*.

Kermit Tyler
Lieutenant, Information Center

" They wanted me to come in [to the Information Center at Fort Shafter] on Sunday morning from 4:00 to 8:00. When I got there, nothing was happening, so I wrote letters and read *Reader's Digest.* I didn't do anything else. It was quiet.

A few plots showed up [on radar] starting about 6:15, which could very well have been Japanese scout planes. They came in and we plotted them, but there was no way of telling what they were. The problem was, we had no identification people on staff yet. A little after 7:00, one of the plotters came up to the balcony and started doing some work on a drafting board. He showed me that at 7:02 there was a plot at 132 miles and three degrees east of north. I had no way of knowing what it was. It made me think that it was probably B-17s, because as I was coming into town, I had flipped on the radio and heard Hawaiian music. A bomber pilot friend of mine had told me, 'When our B-17s are coming in, they play Hawaiian music without interruption so they can home in.' It turned out that the Japanese used the music to home in, too.

At about 7:15 I got a call from Pvt. Joseph Lockard that he had the same plot. He said it was the biggest plot he had ever seen. Well, 12 B-17s could make a pretty big splash on his screen. I told him, 'Don't worry about it. It's O.K.' So that was the end of that. He hung up and I hung up.

After that, not a thing. A few minutes after 8:00 I stepped outside to take a breath of fresh air. I looked off to the west and saw puffs of smoke and a few planes. It looked like they were practicing dive-bombing. It turned out it was the attack. A few minutes later I had a call from a sergeant in operations at Wheeler Field that they had been attacked.

By that time they had the ships burning. We could see the carnage. You just felt like the world was ending. I had the distinct feeling that one of the bombs was going to land on this Information Center because it was such a well-planned attack and they hit everything at once. It was just unbelievable, overwhelming. I have never before or since been so devastated.

I have thought over the years that maybe no one in history has been at a more crucial point. I did my job except for this one thing I felt I was at fault: I didn't take the opportunity to talk at greater length to Lockard about the radar, and what made him think this was anything important. I dropped the ball to the extent that I didn't do that. Whether that would have turned me around and made me alarmed enough to sound an alert, I don't know. If I had passed on the information at 7:15 to Major Bergquist, he would have had to sort out the thing again. What would he do? Would he call an alert? What he would have done is conjecture.

I didn't ever feel what I did could have prevented Pearl Harbor. If we had been on alert, we might have blunted it a bit. But from a standing start like we were, we could not have done very much.

I may have been held back because of Pearl Harbor. I was kind of unlucky to be in the place I was in. I felt that I must have been earmarked to not get very far up the line. Some of the pilots I knew came to me after the attack. They knew I felt bad about it. But they would have done the same thing.

I spoke at the 50th anniversary of the attack. I am real glad that I did. I was able to state things the way they were. I got a lot of sympathy after that, rather than being run down. **"**

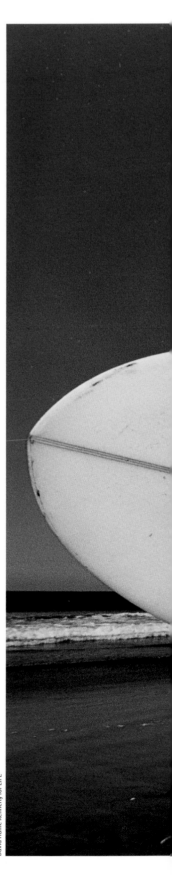

Tyler, with one day's experience at Fort Shafter's Information Center, was the only officer on duty the morning of December 7, 1941. After the war he continued his career in Utah and in England before retiring from the Air Force as a lieutenant colonel in 1961. He settled in San Diego and managed real estate. At 88, he has four kids and three grandchildren—all of whom he has taught to surf.

Taylor served in the Navy until December 1945. A retired California Superior Court judge, he lives in Davis with his wife, Eiko, a native of Japan who came to the U.S. in 1953. They were married in 1977. Taylor, 81, has written a book based on his war experiences and is in the process of finding a publisher. An avid gardener, one of his creations was named Queen of the 1988 National Chrysanthemum Show.

Warren K. Taylor

Ensign, USS *Sumner*

" I was an ensign on the *Sumner,* a survey ship. We were at the Submarine Base, at a dock in front of the administration building. The first thing that we knew, the officer of the deck said there were planes dropping bombs. I ran up onto the fantail. The torpedo planes were coming down East Loch, which was perpendicular to Battleship Row. They needed the long approach to drop their torpedoes. They were flying slowly, and lowly.

If this was a drill, it was a hell of a drill. A little bit later, the first message we received was, 'This is not a drill.'

The first thing I saw was a torpedo plane, which had a red sun and corps insignia. They were paying no attention to us, but they must have been only 100 or 200 yards from us, very close. I had been in the Navy only six weeks—I thought this was a game, the reds against the blues.

General quarters was sounded. I went to my station. I was a supply officer and could type, so I was at a coding board. My job was coding and decoding messages—cryptography. From my post I could see things exploding.

We had primitive antiaircraft guns on the *Sumner,* old-fashioned and ineffective. But one of the guns on the fantail shot down one of the torpedo planes. It was only about 8:00 or 8:05. We almost got another. The gun was just in front of me. The shell missed by three or four feet. A communications officer later told me that we were given credit for being the first ship to shoot down a Japanese plane, although a shore battery did receive credit for having shot one down earlier.

We weren't far from the dry dock where the *Pennsylvania* was. The destroyers *Cassin* and *Downes* had been hit. Their seams were opened up, oil was spilling out, and the oil was on fire. The shells were pirouetting through the air. It was spectacular, like the Fourth of July.

It was all over very quickly. Then the Japanese planes left. And then, after the horse was out of the barn, it was worth your life to walk around that base. You were challenged every hundred yards. The sentries would say, 'Halt! Identify yourself.'

That night a squadron of our planes flew in, and the ships opened fire on them, and the skies were full of tracer bullets. Of course, it was a cathartic moment for the ships.

I can tell you that I was scared to death. I thought I had about five minutes to live. I didn't know it would be another 60 years.

I was one frightened man. "

Ronald Oba
High School Student

"Before the war, the Japanese on Hawaii were mostly immigrants working for the sugar plantations. They had come to make some money and return to Japan. We had many little towns—a Japanese village, a Philippine camp, a Chinese camp, a Portuguese camp, a Spanish camp. We had all kinds of people and got along really well, except for the Caucasians. They always had their own section with their tennis courts and swimming pools.

My parents had arrived around 1914. They ran a barber shop, and I and my six brothers and sisters grew up in Oahu about a quarter of a mile from the north shore of Pearl Harbor. On weekends, we went hiking up the mountains and picked guavas and fruits. We used to swim and fish in Pearl Harbor. At that time there were no restrictions about rowing your boat next to a submarine or a destroyer.

On Sundays, we always had hot cakes. It was a treat. All of a sudden I heard this 'Bang-bang-bang.' It went from one end of the horizon to the other. 'Boom, boom!' I said to my family, 'Oh, they are having maneuvers again.' Then there was a 'rhruunmp' and a great explosion shook our flimsy home.

Still in my pajamas, I jumped up and ran down to the shore. I was there in five minutes. The water was lapping my feet as I was watching. I said, 'My God, the battleship *Arizona* is on fire.' Another battleship started to burn. Early in the morning there is no wind, and the black clouds and the smoke were just going straight up like a mushroom.

I said, 'What is happening?' I looked up and saw swarms of Zeros in the air. I couldn't even hear the drone of the planes because there were so many explosions. I saw a dive-bomber coming from the Waikiki area into Battleship Row. I actually saw it drop a torpedo. Instead of pulling up, the bomber turned and hugged the surface of the water and came directly at me. I saw the pilot's face—he had a canvas type of a helmet and large goggles. He was looking down at me. I was very angry.

Then I saw a couple of Zeros crash in the forest above us. People went to take a look. The pilot was burned to a crisp. As they pulled the body out, a map fell out of his jacket. Every target was circled in red.

As I was standing on shore, a truckload of Marines came up. They yelled at me to go home. I ran back home and they secured the beaches.

That night every house had to be blacked out. If a single ray of light came out, then the house was shot at. Everybody was so scared. Our parents were so afraid, they burned everything that had to do with Japan—the emperor's photo, the Japanese flag. Samurai swords were buried under the house. We had shortwave radios, and were told to break them up. We made a bonfire in the yard and were burning and burying things.

The next day ships were coming back and forth, unloading dead bodies. There was a concrete pier. The sailors' bodies were piled high like cords.

We were immediately charged as enemy aliens. Any Japanese, whether American or not, was declared an enemy alien.

Eventually I went to work for the Navy, building ammunition magazines. I fought with the Japanese-American 442nd regimental combat team in Italy and France. Every parent told us not to come back home—to uphold the *samurai-boshito* upbringing by dying gloriously. They said, 'You don't bring shame to the family. You fight and die in the front lines.'"

After the war Oba earned a master's in hospital administration and oversaw Hilo Hospital on the Big Island until retiring in 1987. Now 79, he edits the 442nd's bulletin, *Go for Broke*. He remembers when, as a young man, he was told by a policeman that he had to enlist to prove himself. Oba still bristles at the implication of disloyalty: "I didn't take kindly to his words. I am an American."

Kay and Frank Tremaine
Civilians

Frank: We arrived in Honolulu in June of 1940 when the United Press news service transferred me there to run its two-man bureau. The military was already getting quite active in Hawaii. It was bustling. We lived in a rented, modest two-story guest house surrounded by palm and mango trees. It had views of Honolulu and Pearl Harbor.

Kay: The night of December 6, we went to a black-tie dinner dance at the Fort DeRussey Officer's Club on Waikiki Beach. Before going home, four of us walked outside. It was a balmy night. There were these heat flashes. It looked like shelling was going on. Commander [George] Gelley made the prophetic remark, 'Just like the calm before the storm.'

Frank: Early in the morning I was awakened by antiaircraft firing, growing and growing in intensity. When I got to the windows I could see puffs in the air out toward Pearl. On a hunch I called the Army headquarters at Fort Shafter. A friend of mine, Harry Albright, was the press officer. I said, 'Harry, you know what is going on?' He said, 'You can say we are under attack.' I said, 'Who is it, Harry? You don't think it is the Germans, do you?'

Kay: What woke me was, Frank rushed through and knocked my dress down. It was a brand-new, very expensive dress my mother had sent from San Francisco, and he was walking back and forth on top of it.

Frank: Kay turned on the radio. A friend of ours named Webley Edwards was on the air saying, 'This is an air raid, this is no drill. Take cover.' I got on the phone. As soon as I sent as many messages as I could, reporting what I had seen and what I had found out, I threw on some clothes. Off I went.

Kay: It is funny how a woman reacts. The first thing I did was grab all our soiled clothes and rush to the garage, so that if the Japs took over and our water supply was polluted, we would have clean things. Then I went back to the house. A crowd had gathered around the swimming pool and was looking out toward Pearl. We had the best view. I heard that siren sound of a falling bomb that they always used in the movies. It hit the side of the hill, and a fragment grazed the forehead of a man standing by the pool. It was one of our own antiaircraft shells.

Frank: I tried to get to Pearl. Traffic was a horrible mess. I got out of line and drove down the other side of the highway, hoping I didn't meet anybody coming in the other direction. Hickam Field is right next to Pearl Harbor. I decided I would go in there. I could see barracks that had taken a lot of hits. There was extensive damage to aircraft along the edge of the field. There were wounded. I phoned three or four times to the bureau to report what I was seeing. A little bit after 11, I was on my fourth call and was told, 'You might as well hold it now. The Navy has cut off all communications.' By the time I got into town it was all pretty quiet.

Kay: There were rumors all day saying that Japanese were landing in the hills above us. All kinds of things, all false. One of the smartest things I did was make a big batch of eggnog. The egg and the milk settled our stomachs, and the alcohol settled our nerves—we didn't know if the attack was coming back or not. You don't realize how quickly the sun goes down out there, and all of a sudden we were caught by darkness. We didn't dare even light a flame on the stove to cook. Here we were just a target right on top of this hill. But nothing came.

Frank: Far as I know, I was the first newsman to see what had happened. I never thought of Pearl in terms of history-making, not until a long time later. As life goes on and people ask me about these things, I sort of step away and see it more as a historic event than a big exciting day in our lives.

Married the day after the September 1, 1939, German blitzkrieg of Poland, the Tremaines spent the duration of the war working throughout the Pacific. Frank remained with a news bureau that ballooned from two to 30 reporters, while Kay worked for the Army as a cryptographer, and then for the *Advertiser* as a journalist. After more than 60 years of marriage, the Tremaines now live in Georgia.

In 1941, McIntosh was writing for both the *Star-Bulletin* and the Scripps-Howard News Service. Later in the war she worked for the OSS in China; afterward she was employed variously by Voice of America, the U.N. and the CIA. At 86, she rides dirt bikes with her husband on their property in Leesburg, Va.

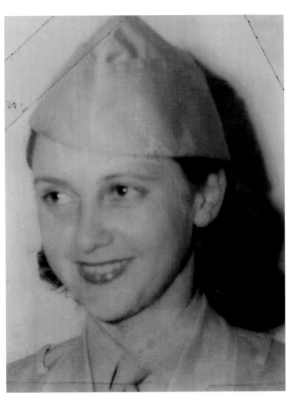

Elizabeth McIntosh
Reporter, *Honolulu Star-Bulletin*

"I got up early and put on the radio. It was the Mormon Tabernacle Choir. All of a sudden this man's voice crackled over and said, 'The islands are under attack. This is the real McCoy.' Then the radio went off and I said, 'Oh, more war games.' The military was always doing games. They would pretend to be attacking the island. I then got a phone call from my photographer, 'Hump' Campbell. He asked if I would like to come on in: 'There's something happening. I'm not sure what.'

On the way in, no one was tense or anything. We were going along wonderful sunny streets. People were walking their dogs or going to church. Some people were playing tennis or shopping. It was an every-Sunday type of leisurely morning.

That all changed when we arrived in Honolulu. We heard sirens. We could feel the tenseness. There was nobody in the streets. First thing we found was an open market filled with Christmas stuff. Antiaircraft shells had knocked it flat. There were tinsel, ribbons, cards and toys around. In the middle of it was this little kid. He was having a wonderful time with all these toys.

It was madness at the *Star-Bulletin*. I asked to be assigned to Pearl. They said, 'No, women are not allowed to go out there.' I was assigned to go to Queens Hospital. At that point the nurses and doctors were putting tape on the windows because they were afraid there might be more bombing. The first people who came in were the Hickam Field firemen. I can just see them, being carried in on stretchers, coming down this long corridor. They were blackened and bleeding. A lot of the men were unconscious. Some of them were groaning. I tried to talk to them, but they didn't seem to want to talk about whatever had happened to them.

There was also a little girl that they brought in. She had a jump rope. The rope had been burned, and she was just holding the handles in her hands. She was about five or six. She was all burned and I don't think she lived. It was just awful.

This was around 10 o'clock. I stayed there all day getting stories, then walked back to the office. There was just complete desolation: The whole city was closed down except for the police and the sirens.

I got the stuff out for Scripps-Howard papers, but then found out that the censorship had set in and you could not send anything by wire out of Honolulu. All the people were afraid that the Japanese were going to really invade. There were rumors that they were coming in the mountains, and that they were sending troops to cover the whole island. We had people from the *Bulletin* who were afraid to go home. That night, after we put the paper to bed, they asked if they could go with me. So a whole bunch spent the night with me and drank all my Scotch.

I got out to Pearl a couple of days later. All along the streets there were dead mynah birds and doves and sparrows. The concussion from the bombs had killed them. At Pearl it was horrible—that whole awful scene. There was oil in the water, and the smell. The buildings all flattened and rubble. The ships so silent. I remember, at the *Arizona*, the air bubbles bubbling up from below. It could have been people. There were 1,000 men or something like that down below. And all the oil and the smell that you could still smell from the bombs."

Charles Merdinger
Ensign, USS *Nevada*

Merdinger served on the *Alabama* during the war; afterward he won a Rhodes Scholarship and earned a doctorate from Oxford. He continued with the Navy's CEC/Seabees through the Korean and Vietnam conflicts, retiring from the service as a captain in 1970. He became president of Washington College and deputy director of Scripps Oceanography. Now 83, he and his wife, Mary, live in Nevada.

"I was ashore that Saturday and got this little tree. It was going to brighten up our little cabin for Christmas. On Sunday, all of a sudden I heard general quarters and the bugle. I got out of my pajamas and got through my second sock when a fellow ran by my room and yelled, 'It's the real thing.' There was a huge explosion and machine-gun fire. I went right to my battle station, which was further down. I ran the range keeper, which calculated how the big guns should be trained and fired. Since we were not going to shoot 14-inch guns at planes, our station became a sort of central communications area.

There had been so many people wounded up above on the five-inch guns that they needed relief. I was told to send half of the men immediately. I just looked around and figured out which were the least important phone lines being manned. I picked those people and told them to go. It was 'Aye, aye, sir.' Nobody wanted to take a vote or discuss the matter or philosophize about it.

Soon after the attack, the *Nevada* got under way. Then the Japs really jumped us. They must have hit us a couple of times in the course of that run in the channel. The ship was beginning to tilt, going down. We were ordered to beach the ship to keep the channel clear. The ship settled down and the main deck almost was awash, a foot or two from the surface.

Our room was relatively calm and quiet. There was no sense of panic. When the main power went out, I told everyone to lie down on the deck to conserve air. Most of us removed our shirts or opened them because it was kind of hot. We didn't really have any change of air down there.

Late in the day, water began to drip from overhead. That was the first inkling we had that we were basically in an air bubble. Then the gaskets on the door by which we entered started to give way, and the water started coming in. It was a couple of inches, up around our ankles. It never occurred to me at the time how we were going to get out. When the water came in the door, I realized that we were really in for it. I called up the executive officer and requested permission to secure. He said, 'Permission granted.' I told everybody we were going to secure. There was no mad rush. I opened the other door to the next room, and everybody filed out. We had been in there from eight in the morning till about three in the afternoon.

I recall bodies lying around in the other room, and it being smoky. I went up a couple of decks and smelled fresh air. That was the most magnificent breath of air I ever took. When I got out and looked around, the whole world was on fire. Ships were burning and oil on the water was on fire. My first reaction was 'Lord, thanks that I made it out in one piece.' The other was, 'These Japs really did a professional job.'

I looked around the deck. People were running around and it was kind of a shambles. Everybody was concerned that there would be more attacks. They had no idea what was out there.

After it got dark, we still manned our guns. Planes were coming into port. We knew they were friendly, and the gunnery officer yelled to everybody, 'Hold your fire. Don't do anything.' But some bird let go with a machine gun, and the next thing you know the whole harbor erupted into this cone of fire. The tracers made an umbrella of fire—360 degrees. I guess we shot down a couple of them. They were our own people, and here we were just firing madly. It was one of those horrible things."

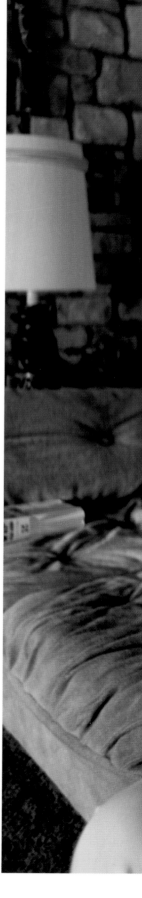

After the attack, Emory worked on convoys to Australia, was at the Battle of Tassafaronga, then served on an amphibious transport. He left the service in 1946, worked as a mechanical engineer, and moved back to Honolulu 16 years ago (he is pictured below walking in the Punchbowl graveyard among the Pearl Harbor dead). Now 80, he is a historian for the Pearl Harbor Survivors Association.

Raymond Emory
Seaman, USS *Honolulu*

"I can remember it like it was just yesterday. I was reading a newspaper at my bunk, one deck below topside. General quarters sounded. Naturally everybody headed for their battle stations. I got to the .50-caliber machine guns. I was the first one there and started pulling the covers off. I had one all of the way off and another about halfway off when the first plane went by our stern. When the second plane went by, I noticed the big red ball. That was when I realized what was going on.

The ammunition box was locked at the machine gun. I didn't know who had the keys and didn't care anyway. I just had to get the damn thing opened. I used a dog wrench, a piece of pipe, to break the box open. After we got the box open and the machine guns manned, we fired at anything that came close.

When you are firing a machine gun you kind of get tunnel vision. You are concentrating on what you are firing at, and you are not seeing anything to the left or right. I only saw this one plane go down: The prop came off of the nose and kept on going, but the torpedo plane just stopped in the mid-

dle of the air, lit like a Christmas tree, and down it went. That was the only airplane I saw go down, and everybody and his brother were firing at it.

The only noise that I remember was a three-inch gun right below us. When that thing went, I never heard anything else. When a big bang goes off near your ears, you don't hear for quite a while. I never heard the *Arizona* blowing up, or anything else.

Soon as the attack was over, we didn't just stop shooting and then stand around. The adrenaline was flowing. We were back down in the magazine getting more ammunition, getting ready for the next wave. The Japanese came back after about half an hour. They stuck around a bit longer than the first wave. When the second wave came in, one bomb came at the *Honolulu* and was a near miss and hit the dock. It went down through the concrete before it went off. It caved the side of the ship in about four feet deep and about 20 feet high. The water flooded the magazines the same time it got hit.

Then there was hardly anything on our side of the ship to fire at. It was all over on the other side. We could see them hit Hickam Field, but they were just out of our range.

We stayed at our battle stations the rest of the day and all night. We were concerned, but I wasn't scared. There were all kinds of rumors around. Aircraft carriers out five miles, 10 miles. Paratroopers landing. Amphibious transports out there. The Japanese were all going to make a landing. Rumors flew like you would not believe. My concern that morning was where they had come from to get here so fast, and who declared war on who first.

Today, there are so many stories being told that it is pathetic. All you hear out here when you go to the memorial is '*Arizona, Arizona, Arizona.*' People don't realize that there were other ships. I don't think the majority of people even care.

As for the Japanese—the way the Japanese government was back then and the way it is even today is totally different than the way we live. Totally.

If my neighbor raped and murdered my mother 50 years ago, I sure as hell wouldn't be inviting him for lunch. That is just the way I feel."

Dana Edmunds for LIFE

This view of Battleship Row symbolizes the beginning and end of America's involvement in WW II. The USS *Missouri*, on which the Japanese formally surrendered, moved to the Row in 1998. A ship's length ahead of "Mighty Mo" lies the USS Arizona Memorial. Opposite: Nearly half the Americans who died at Pearl Harbor are buried at Punchbowl, the National Memorial Cemetery of the Pacific, in the crater of an extinct volcano.

PEARL HARBOR TODAY

The serene bay was once known for the pearl oysters that grew in its waters. Since the late 1800s, when Hawaii's King Kalakaua gave the U.S. permission to develop there, the area has been known as a base of naval operations. Since December 7, 1941, the harbor has been known for one thing above all. This year, on the 60th anniversary of the infamous date, we pause once more to remember Pearl Harbor.

Marc Schechter/Photo Resource Hawaii

Peter French

These photographs were taken at the Arizona Memorial. The clock above, which was salvaged from the ship in 1942, reflects forever a heartbreaking moment. The names of the 1,177 sailors and Marines who were lost on the *Arizona* are inscribed on the marble wall at right. It has come to commemorate all military personnel who died during the attack. Visitors to the shrine often float leis in their memory.

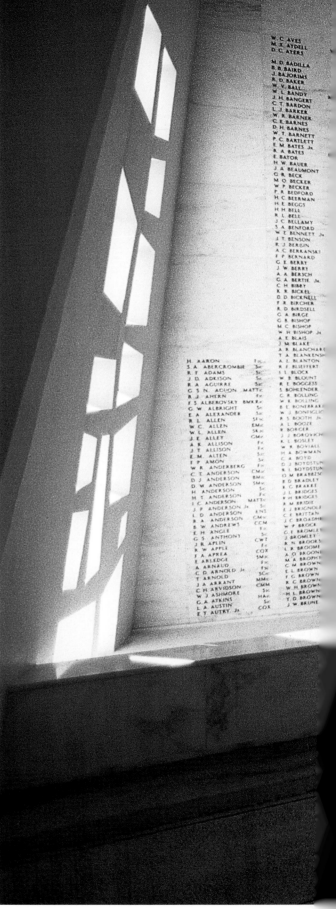

TO THE MEMORY OF THE GALLANT MEN
HERE ENTOMBED AND THEIR SHIPMATES
WHO GAVE THEIR LIVES IN ACTION
ON DECEMBER 7, 1941 ON THE U.S.S. ARIZONA

The idea that there be some kind of testimonial emerged in 1943 but wasn't realized until 1962 with the dedication of the USS Arizona Memorial. The 184-foot-long enclosed bridge spans the hull of the fallen battleship. The monument commemorates all members of the military who died at Pearl Harbor.